# MARGO OLIVER'S
# COOKBOOK FOR SENIORS

## Nutritious recipes for one - two - or more

Margo Oliver

**Self-Counsel Press**
(*a division of*)
International Self-Counsel Press Ltd.
Canada          U.S.A.

*Printed in Canada*

*First edition: May, 1989; Reprinted: October, 1989*

> Canadian Cataloguing in Publication Data
> Oliver, Margo, 1923-
> Margo Oliver's cookbook for seniors
>
> (Self-counsel retirement series)
>            Includes index.
> ISBN 0-88908-695-8
>               1. Cookery.     2. Aged - Nutrition.
>               I. Title.     II. Title: Cookbook for seniors
> III. Series.
> TX715.045 1989     641.5′627     C89-091179-7

*Cover photo by Colin Clarke*

*Illustrations by Janette Lush*

**Self-Counsel Press**
(*a division of*)
International Self-Counsel Press Ltd.
*Head and Editorial Office*
1481 Charlotte Road
North Vancouver, British Columbia V7J 1H1

*U.S. Address*
1704 N. State Street
Bellingham, Washington     98225

# CONTENTS

# PREFACE

*To be seventy years young is sometimes far more
cheerful than to be forty years old.*

Oliver Wendell Holmes

I resent the fact that my dictionary defines "senior
citizen" as "an elderly person." I don't feel elderly, nor
do I feel senior. But, since no one has come up with a
better word than senior for us who are now mature, I
suppose we might as well be philosophical about it —
but let's keep thinking young!

It isn't easy to reach "a certain age" and find, sud-
denly, just the two of you with family grown and gone.
Even worse is to find yourself all on your own. And one
of the difficult things about each of these situations is
dealing with the meals of the day. If you are alone, as I
am now, it's hard to motivate yourself to make a complete meal. And, if there are just two of you, after being
used to a good-sized family, it's difficult to learn to shop
and cook in miniature.

So when I was asked to write this book, it seemed
to me to be important. I didn't plan recipes for special
diets or for people who can't cope in the kitchen very
well. Instead, I thought of myself and so many of my
friends who are healthy (relatively), independent
people of optimistic nature — though over 65!

Thinking about these people made me realize that
those with the most problems are the men who are
living alone and struggling with meals because they
have so little experience with cooking. So I made a
decision that there should be quite a bit of really basic
information here. (Please forgive me all of you good,

experienced cooks.) But, I've also included bits of information I hope will be helpful to *all* senior cooks: things such as equipment needed for cooking in small amounts, a discussion of the most common spices and herbs, equivalents, and a large number of suggested menus, as well as recipes.

Nutrition is something seniors wonder about. Should you eat differently? Basically, if your health is good, the answer is a slightly qualified no. The obvious things you know about: try to avoid salt, fats, and too much sugar; include fiber; and, cut down on calories if you need to. It's too easy to gain weight along with years, so it's important to cram as much nutrition in as few calories as possible. Instead of giving you a lecture on nutrition (but don't forget the four essential food groups: milk and milk products, meats and alternates, bread and cereals, fruit and vegetables), I've given you a small dose at the beginning of each recipe section. There you will find what the various foods contribute toward your good health.

I've tried to plan the recipes so most needs are covered. They range from simple to challenging (noted by one, two, or three symbols: ❦), and there are recipes in the "penny-saving" category as well as others that mean you're ready to spoil yourself a little. There are suggestions for entertaining too — whether just for coffee or a glass of wine with a snack or for special times with dear friends or family.

Mostly, my hope for this book is that it will make cooking for all of us interesting and fun. Even if you haven't done much cooking up to now, you will be surprised what an adventure it can be and what a marvelous hobby it can grow into. To enjoy top quality of life, you must feel good. So take a positive look at cooking and your diet and set out to eat well as part of your regime to promote your good health.

# KITCHEN HELPERS

## EQUIPMENT

You'll find that a lot of the pots, pans, casseroles and even appliances you have (perhaps some you've had since you were first married) aren't suitable for your everyday cooking now. A loaf pan, measuring 9 x 5 x 3 inches, that you used for meat loaf and bread, isn't nearly as useful now as two small (about 5 x 3 x 2-inch) metal or foil pans will be. Small casseroles are needed to replace the larger family ones. Mind you, you can still make some of your smaller casserole recipes, then divide them into two and freeze one for next week. For this type of cooking, I find "cook 'n freeze" foil pans that measure 5 x 4 x 1½ inches and have covers very useful.

Perhaps you are moving into smaller quarters? That means you will really want to clear out as much of the unusable kitchen equipment as possible.

Here is a list of things I find indispensable in my kitchen and a second list of things I find nice to have. (Use the boxes to tick off those items you have as you take an inventory of your kitchen.)

## Indispensable

### General kitchen equipment:

❏ Long-handled kitchen fork

❏ Slotted spoon

❏ Wooden spoons

❏ Turner (for pancakes, eggs, etc.)

❏ Soup ladle

1

- ❏ Potato masher
- ❏ Vegetable peeler with floating blade
- ❏ Rubber scrapers
- ❏ Kitchen shears
- ❏ Egg beater
- ❏ Sieves (small and medium)
- ❏ Graters
- ❏ Tongs
- ❏ Colander
- ❏ Funnel
- ❏ Cutting board
- ❏ Pastry board
- ❏ Rolling pin
- ❏ Bowls (graduated set)
- ❏ Lemon squeezer
- ❏ Steamer

**Knives:**

- ❏ serrated for bread
- ❏ paring
- ❏ medium

**Openers:**

- ❏ can (hand held)
- ❏ jar (the kind that grips hard-to-open jars)
- ❏ bottle
- ❏ corkscrew

**Measuring utensils:**

- ❑ Measuring spoons
- ❑ Glass measuring cup (for liquids)
- ❑ Nest of metal or plastic measuring cups (for dry ingredients)

**Pots and pans:**

- ❑ Saucepans, (heavy, small and medium, with lids
- ❑ Heavy frying pan, with lid if possible
- ❑ Dutch oven

**Small casseroles:**

- ❑ 2 x 20 oz. (500 mL)
- ❑ 2 x 1 qt. (1 L)
- ❑ 1½ qt. (1.5 L)

**Bakeware:**

- ❑ Loaf pans (at least two), metal or foil, about 5½ x 3¼ x 2 inches
- ❑ Foil pie pans — 4½ inches in diameter
- ❑ Glass pie pan — 9 inches in diameter
- ❑ Custard cups — 6 oz. (200 mL)
- ❑ Square cake pan — 8 x 8 x 2 inches
- ❑ Small cookie sheet
- ❑ Muffin tin (six or eight cups)
- ❑ Small roasting pan with rack

**Baking dishes (glass or pottery):**

- ❑ approximately 8 x 6 x 2 inches
- ❑ approximately 12 x 7 x 2 inches

## Electric applicances:

- ❑ Portable electric mixer
- ❑ Blender
- ❑ Toaster oven
- ❑ Tea kettle
- ❑ Coffee maker

## For storage:

- ❑ Canisters
- ❑ Paper towels
- ❑ Aluminum foil (heavy duty for freezing)
- ❑ Freezer bags
- ❑ Storage bags
- ❑ Transparent wrap
- ❑ Waxed paper
- ❑ Plastic cartons with tight lids (storage, refrigerator, freezer)

## Nice to have

- ❑ Wire whip
- ❑ Pastry blender
- ❑ Apple corer
- ❑ Extra timer
- ❑ Biscuit (cookie) cutter
- ❑ Food chopper
- ❑ Chef's knife

- ❏ Grapefruit knife
- ❏ Garlic press
- ❏ Meat thermometer
- ❏ Frying pan (with non-stick surface and sloping sides)
- ❏ Omelet pan
- ❏ Double boiler
- ❏ Stock pot
- ❏ Wok
- ❏ Table model electric mixer
- ❏ Food processor
- ❏ Microwave oven
- ❏ Electric juicer
- ❏ Waffle iron
- ❏ Wooden salad bowl and servers
- ❏ Spinner (for drying salad greens)
- ❏ Cheesecloth
- ❏ Parchment paper

## BASIC SUPPLIES

Suppose it's too stormy to go out, or you aren't feeling as well as you might, or unexpected company arrives on a holiday. Would you be able to prepare a meal? It's important to keep enough things in the cupboard and freezer so you can make a good meal at any time. Here's a list of the supplies I like to keep on hand. (The list doesn't include things that have to be bought often, such as dairy products.)

## Basics

- ❏ Granulated sugar
- ❏ Brown sugar
- ❏ Honey
- ❏ All-purpose flour
- ❏ Whole wheat flour
- ❏ Salt and pepper (whole peppercorns in a pepper mill preferably)
- ❏ Baking powder
- ❏ Baking soda
- ❏ Vanilla extract
- ❏ Vegetable oil
- ❏ Cold cereals
- ❏ Oatmeal or other cereal to cook
- ❏ Rice
- ❏ Pasta
- ❏ Evaporated milk
- ❏ Dry skim milk
- ❏ Cornstarch
- ❏ Chicken, beef, and vegetable bouillon cubes or powder
- ❏ White vinegar
- ❏ Peanut butter
- ❏ Jam
- ❏ Pancake syrup
- ❏ Raisins

- ❑ Nuts
- ❑ Crackers
- ❑ Prepared mustard
- ❑ Coffee
- ❑ Tea
- ❑ Salad dressing
- ❑ Canned tomatoes
- ❑ Canned tomato juice
- ❑ Canned salmon
- ❑ Canned tuna
- ❑ Canned fruit juice
- ❑ Canned pineapple (in its own juice)
- ❑ Bread (in the freezer for emergencies)

## Extras
- ❑ Artificial sweetener
- ❑ Gelatin
- ❑ Olive oil
- ❑ Wine vinegar
- ❑ Soya sauce
- ❑ Worcestershire sauce
- ❑ Ketchup
- ❑ Cocoa
- ❑ Garlic
- ❑ Frozen vegetables
- ❑ Frozen fruit

# HERBS AND SPICES

Important when you are trying to avoid too much salt are the marvelous tastes of herbs and spices. Herbs, of course, come fresh, in dried leaf form, and as powders. Spices may be bought whole, but are usually ground.

**Herbs:** Take care to use a light hand; too little is better than too much. A general rule is one-quarter teaspoon of any dried herb for each four servings to start — then increase as desired the next time. If you are using fresh herbs, you will want to use three or four times as much as dried.

Some of my favorite herbs and suggested uses are given in the box on the opposite page.

**Spices:** As with herbs, a light hand is better than a heavy one. You want to make things taste better, but you don't want to destroy the good flavor of the ingredients you are seasoning. Buy spices in as small quantities as possible. They are often available in bulk food stores, but if you have to buy a whole jar, try to share with a friend because they do lose their flavor over time. Store spices in a cool, dry, dark place.

The spices I find most useful are nutmeg, cinnamon, ginger, whole cloves, chili powder, curry powder, mustard, ground pepper, whole peppercorns, and paprika.

# HERBS AND THEIR USES

| | |
|---|---|
| **Basil** | Tomatoes and tomato dishes, spaghetti sauce, beans, green salad, beef |
| **Bay leaf** | Soup stocks, stews, tomatoes, all meats |
| **Chervil** | Eggs, fish, poultry, salads |
| **Dill** | Green beans, cottage cheese, fish, salads, sauces |
| **Marjoram** | Vegetables, fish, poultry, poultry stuffing |
| **Mint** | Lamb, cold beverages, fruit salads, vegetables |
| **Oregano** | Salad dressings, omelets, meat loaf, veal, pasta sauces |
| **Parsley** | Almost everything except desserts |
| **Rosemary** | Fruit salads, lamb, pork, vegetables, chicken |
| **Sage** | Poultry stuffings, pork, meat loaf |
| **Savory** | Poultry stuffings, stews, hamburgers, eggs, fish, and shellfish |
| **Tarragon** | Fish and shellfish, veal, chicken |
| **Thyme** | Tomatoes, beans, meats, stews, stock |

# A WORD ABOUT METRIC

If you are interested in trying metric recipes, you'll find it easy. All you need is three inexpensive types of metric measures: liquid, dry, and small. (If you've bought a liquid measuring cup in the last few years, it probably shows metric measures on one side.) However, don't try to convert recipes because you may get poor results. You must use metric measures and metric recipes together.

For convenience, I have given all the recipes in this book in the familiar cup and spoon measures. But I'm sure you've noticed that even when cans and packages are marked in metric only, shopping hasn't changed much. Just as a litre of milk doesn't look strange any more, a can of salmon, even though marked in metric, is still a can of familiar size. And since 250 mL (millilitres) is very close to 1 cup, if your recipe calls for ½ cup of sour cream, for example, you will buy a 250 mL carton and use half of it. In the same way, 1 kg (kilogram) is 1000 g (grams) and a little more than 2 pounds. So it's easy. Just buy 500 grams if your meat loaf recipe calls for 1 pound of meat.

Even though in this book I don't worry about cooking the metric way, you might find it fun to try some metric recipes just so you'll understand how well and easily the method works.

# KNOW-HOW FOR NEW COOKS

When we were young, though most girls helped out in the kitchen, most boys didn't. And so it has continued: Most men of retirement age and older have very little experience in making good meals. So, with apologies to both the men and women who are already great cooks, this section tries to fill in some of the basic knowledge to make cooking easier and more fun for new cooks. I've included information on how to measure and what all the abbreviations mean; some useful equivalents to help with buying; a short dictionary of food terms; and information on baking, buying, storing, cooking, and serving cheese, eggs, fish, meat, poultry, and vegetables; cooking rice and pasta; and how to make good tea, coffee, salads, and soups.

## HOW TO MEASURE

When you are learning to cook it is important to follow recipes, and to follow recipes you need to use the proper measuring utensils correctly. In the list of indispensable kitchen equipment in the first section, I suggested measuring spoons, a glass measuring cup for liquid, and a nest of metal or plastic measuring cups for dry ingredients. The measuring spoons come in 1 tablespoon, 1 teaspoon, ½ teaspoon, and ¼ teaspoon sizes and can be used for liquid or dry ingredients. For thick liquids and dry ingredients, overfill the spoon and level off with the back of a knife. The cup for liquids (I find the 2-cup glass cup the most useful) gives you space above the top measuring line so you can fill to the line without the liquid running over. The nested dry cups come in 1-cup, ½-cup, ⅓-cup, and ¼-cup sizes. All

11

dry ingredients, shortening, and thick liquids (such as molasses) are measured in these. Flour and granulated sugar can be spooned into cups to overfill, then leveled off. Solid fats and brown sugar should be packed into cups, then leveled. Cheese should be packed down lightly.

## LEARNING THE ABBREVIATIONS

Here are the most commonly used abbreviations:

| | |
|---|---|
| tablespoon | tbsp. |
| teaspoon | tsp. |
| pound | lb. |
| ounce | oz. |
| litre | L |
| millilitre | mL |
| kilogram | kg |
| gram | g |

**Equivalent Measures**

| | |
|---|---|
| 3 tsp. | 1 tbsp. |
| 4 tbsp. | ¼ cup |
| 5 tbsp. + 1 tsp. | ⅓ cup |
| 8 tbsp. | ½ cup |
| 12 tbsp. | ¾ cup |
| 16 tbsp. | 1 cup |
| 1 cup | 8 oz. |

# A FEW USEFUL EQUIVALENTS

| | | | |
|---|---|---|---|
| Apples | 1 lb. | 3 med. | 3 cups sliced |
| Banana | | 1 med. | ⅓ cup mashed |
| Lemon | | 1 med. | 3 tbsp. juice<br>2 tsp. grated rind |
| Orange | | 1 med. | ⅓ cup juice<br>1 tbsp. grated rind |
| Macaroni | 1 cup (4 oz.) | | 2 cups cooked |
| Noodles | 1 cup (2½ oz.) | | 1¼ cups cooked |
| Spaghetti | 1 cup (4 oz.) | | 2 cups cooked |
| Rice (regular) | 1 cup (7 oz.) | | 3 to 3½ cups cooked |
| Rice (quick) | 1 cup (3 oz.) | | 2 cups cooked |
| Cabbage | 1 small | | 5 cups shredded or finely chopped |
| Onion | | 1 med. | ½ cup chopped |
| Cheese (cheddar) | 4 oz. | | 1 cup grated |
| Egg | | 1 large | 3 tbsp. lightly beaten |
| Cream, whipping | 1 cup | | 2 cups whipped |
| Flour, all-purpose | 1 lb. | | 4 cups sifted |
| Flour, whole wheat | 1 lb. | | 3 ½ cups |
| Sugar, granulated | 1 lb. | | 2 cups |
| Sugar, brown | 1 lb. | | 2 ¼ cups packed |
| Sugar, icing | 1 lb. | | 3 ½ cups sifted |

# DICTIONARY OF SOME FOOD TERMS

**Baste:** Moisten food while cooking by spooning or brushing liquid over top.

**Boil:** Cook in bubbling liquid.

**Braise:** Brown in a little fat, then cover and cook in a small amount of liquid.

**Broil:** Cook tender meats on rack in pan close under heat.

**Cream:** Rub shortening and sugar together with the back of a spoon or beat with mixer until blended and creamy.

**Cut in:** Use a pastry blender or two knives cutting against each other to incorporate shortening into flour mixture.

**Cube:** Cut in cubes usually ¼ to ½ inch.

**Dice:** Cut in very small cubes.

**Dredge:** Coat on all sides with flour or seasoned flour.

**Flake:** Break carefully into small pieces as with canned salmon.

**Fry:** Pan fry in a small amount of fat.

**Grate:** Shred by rubbing over a grater as with cheese.

**Knead:** Press dough with heel of hand, folding over and turning after each press.

**Marinate:** Let food stand in some mixture for added flavor and/or tenderness.

**Mince:** Chop into very small pieces.

**Poach:** Cook by setting in simmering liquid (see simmer).

**Purée:** Press cooked food through a sieve, or use a blender or food processor, to make a smooth mixture.

**Roast:** Cook by dry heat — usually in oven.

**Sauté:** Brown and cook in a small amount of fat in a skillet.

**Scald:** Heat to a temperature just below boiling.

**Sear:** Brown surface of meat quickly.

**Simmer:** Cook in hot liquid that is just below boiling point.

**Steam:** Cook, covered, on steamer or rack over the steam that rises from boiling water.

**Stew:** Cook slowly in liquid for a long time.

**Toss:** Mix lightly without bruising ingredients.

**Whip:** Beat rapidly with egg beater or mixer until thick (for cream) or stiff (for egg whites).

## BASICS OF BAKING

I've already said that measuring is important for a new cook. Nowhere is it more important than in baking. Perhaps you think you won't want to do much baking but, somewhere along the line, you'll probably want to make muffins or pancakes or hot biscuits. It's best to read the recipe right through before you begin, then to get out the ingredients and utensils you need and set your oven temperature.

The ingredients most used in baking are flour, sugar, fat, eggs, leavening, and liquid. You may find you have little use for anything but all-purpose flour, which, today, is enriched so is perfectly nutritious. However, thinking of the fiber you should get in your diet, a small bag of whole wheat flour (it makes wonderful pancakes and quick breads), kept in the refrigerator or freezer, is nice to have. Unless you plan to use the whole wheat flour immediately, it should be kept cold because it contains all of the wheat berry, including the wheat germ, and can go rancid.

You are sure to have granulated sugar on hand and honey is sometimes nice as a sweetener. Brown sugar adds flavor to baking. Keep it in a tight glass container so it stays moist. If it should dry out and become hard, just set a quarter of an apple on a piece of waxed paper in the container for a day or two. It softens the sugar like magic!

The fats you likely have on hand are butter or margarine and probably some vegetable oil. If you intend to do a lot of baking, you may want to have vegetable shortening too.

Leavenings include baking powder, baking soda, yeast, and eggs. There are reasonably small packages of baking powder and soda available, but if you don't use them fairly often, try to share them with a friend because they lose their potency with time.

Liquid can be many things, but milk is most commonly used in baking. I find I can use whole milk, 2% milk, and skim milk interchangeably in most recipes. If a recipe calls for buttermilk or soured milk, you can sour it by adding one tablespoon of white vinegar for each cup of milk. Do not use milk that has gone sour — it is spoiled. Many baking recipes call for the pans to be greased. Shortening is best for greasing; butter or oil may cause sticking.

Pans can make a difference in the browning of your baked things. For bread and pastry (with little or no sugar) dark metal or glass pans work well. They make the bread crusty and brown the pastry well because the pans absorb heat. However, if you are baking cookies, cake, or sweet quick breads, shiny pans are best. They reflect the heat away so things don't brown too much.

Something I've found useful since I've been on my own is making up a large batch of biscuit mix. The mix can be used for hot biscuits, muffins, quick breads, meat pie toppings, shortcake biscuits, etc. A basic biscuit mix recipe is given on page 174.

## BEVERAGES

### Coffee

An important thing in many people's lives is their morning coffee and a nice cuppa tea. I love coffee and find I make it stronger and stronger — though I shouldn't. I compensate for that by adding a large amount of hot skim milk. It's good!

To make good coffee be sure your coffeepot is clean. An automatic pot will come with manufacturer's directions for cleaning periodically. In any case, pots should be washed with hot soapy water and rinsed very well after each use. Using fresh, cold water and fresh coffee is important too. It is really worthwhile, if you are a real coffee lover, to buy a small grinder so you can grind the beans you like as you need them. There are also small coffee makers available. My smallest makes four cups. If you are like me, however, and can't resist making a full large pot in the morning just in case someone drops in, try storing the brewed coffee in a thermos. It stays hot all day but doesn't get an overbrewed taste.

Decaffeinated coffee has become more and more popular as the quality has improved. I am not bothered by caffeine, but I find many of my friends wouldn't think of drinking anything but decaffeinated in the evening, so I habitually make it after a dinner party.

If you buy coffee beans, be sure to buy Arabica rather than Robusta. Arabica is more expensive but has far less caffeine and much more flavor.

The amount of coffee to use per serving naturally depends on how strong you like it. Two to three level tablespoons per serving is a good rule.

## Tea

To make good tea, you need to heat a very clean teapot with boiling water. Use only fresh, cold water and bring it to a full boil. Empty the teapot when it is hot, add the tea to the pot (one teaspoon loose tea for each cup plus one for the pot or one tea bag for each two cups) and pour in the boiling water (three-quarter cup measure for each teacupful of tea). Stir and let steep three to five minutes. Strain or remove tea bags and serve with milk or lemon.

## CHEESE

Natural cheese is made by coagulating milk proteins then separating the solid part (curds) from the liquid (whey). The curd becomes the cheese and the distinctive flavors of different cheeses are due to the naturally developed acids and enzymes and micro-organisms in the cheese and to the time and temperature of storage.

Unripened cheese is the simplest type of all and includes cottage, ricotta, pot, farmers, and fresh cream cheese. Ripened cheeses start out the same way as all cheese, but then they are stored under controlled temperature and humidity to ripen for different periods of time to develop a certain flavor. Some cheeses, particularly the "blues," have mold added, which gives them their blue veins and very distinctive flavor. The cheeses with "holes," like Emmentaler, have a special organism added.

Process cheese is made from cheddar, cream, or other cheese alone or in combination. The cheeses are ground, melted, pasteurized, and then blended. Process cheese melts easily for cooking, but some flavor is lost since pasteurization stops further ripening.

Well-aged natural cheeses usually cost more than the milder, less-aged ones. Imported cheeses are likely to cost more than domestic. It's a good idea to check the prices of store brands against brand names for the best buy.

Store all cheese well wrapped and in the refrigerator. Soft cheese should be used as soon as possible but hard cheese will keep several months. While surface mold can be cut or scraped off, if the mold penetrates deeply into the cheese it should be discarded.

If a piece of cheese dries out by accident, just grate it and store it in a jar with a tight lid in the refrigerator or freezer to use for tops of casseroles, sauces, etc. It's usually not a good idea to freeze pieces of cheese because they become crumbly, but if you must freeze, wrap pieces tightly in heavy-duty foil and freeze no longer than six months.

All cheese, except cottage, should be allowed to warm to room temperature for at least 30 minutes before serving.

Cheese should always be cooked at a low heat to prevent toughening, stringing, and separating.

## EGGS

For general use I find large eggs (rather than medium or extra large) most useful. Most recipes are tested with large eggs. There is no difference in flavor or goodness between white and brown eggs. Fresh eggs, when broken, show a thick white and a yolk that stands up nicely rounded. Eggs should be refrigerated at all times.

**To Soft Cook Eggs in the Shell:** Cover the eggs in a small deep saucepan with cold water, at least one inch above the eggs. Set over high heat and bring to a boil, uncovered, then remove from the heat, cover, and let stand two to four minutes.

**To Hard Cook Eggs in the Shell:** Follow the directions for soft cooking except let stand, covered and off the heat, 20 minutes. Run under cold water for several minutes to cool. Using this method, you'll find you won't get a dark ring around the yolk.

**To Poach Eggs:** Put two inches of water in a deep skillet or saucepan and heat to boiling. Add one tablespoon white vinegar and reduce heat so water is just simmering. Break each egg into a small dish (a custard cup works well) and, holding the dish near the water surface, slip each egg into the water. Cover and simmer three minutes for soft poached and five minutes if you like the yolk hard.

**To Scramble Eggs:** With a fork, lightly mix together eggs and one tablespoon milk for each egg. Add a little salt and pepper. Heat one and a half teaspoons butter or margarine for each two eggs in a skillet over medium heat until it sizzles. Pour in the egg mixture and reduce heat to low. As egg begins to set, lift and fold it so the liquid part can run underneath. Remove from heat when set but still moist and glossy, about three minutes.

## FISH

Now that you can buy good fresh fish almost everywhere, you can enjoy its delicious flavor and delicate texture. It gives variety to menus, supplies good quality protein, and, since it is easily digested, it is suitable for everyone's diet.

Fatty fish include salmon, sardines, mackerel, herring, lake trout, tuna, and turbot. Halibut and whitefish are considered average in fat; for those of you who are looking for low calorie meals, there is a good range of lean fish which, if cooked without added fat, fills the bill gloriously. The lean fish include sole, haddock, cod, ocean perch, fresh water perch, pike, pickerel or walleye (doré), and smelt.

**Buying Fresh Fish:** Try to find out from your fish store (or supermarket) when the fresh fish is received — then buy and cook it that day. Fresh fish has red gills and bright and tight scales. The flesh is firm to touch and any aroma should be fresh and natural — not "fishy." Really fresh fish has almost no odor. Allow one pound per serving for whole fish and one pound per two or three servings for cleaned, ready-to-eat fish.

**Buying Frozen Fish:** Since most frozen fish in supermarkets is hidden in sealed packages, you have to rely on brands you know and hope the store takes good care of its frozen food counter. Packaged frozen fish comes in several forms including solid fillet blocks, individually wrapped fillets (good for us loners), and breaded portions.

**Storing Fish:** If possible, fresh fish should not be stored at all. It should be bought, brought home, and cooked immediately. If it must be kept, do not keep it longer than one day. Wash it in cold water, pat dry with paper towels, wrap in waxed paper, and store in the coldest part of the refrigerator.

Frozen fish should be bought at the end of the shopping expedition and brought home and stored in the freezer in its original wrapping until needed. Do not refreeze fish that has thawed.

**Cooking Fish:** The basic ways to cook fish are pan or oven frying, broiling, steaming, deep fat frying, baking, and poaching. For the health of your digestive system, you do best to broil, bake, steam, or poach. No matter which method you use, it is important not to overcook. Fish is done when it becomes opaque and flakes easily with a fork. The 10-Minute Rule is a good one to remember: *Allow 10 minutes total cooking time per inch of thickness (at thickest point) for fresh fish, 20 minutes for frozen fish.*

If possible, it's best to cook frozen fish without thawing it first (unless you are microwaving, in which case fish should be thoroughly thawed). However, you'll have to partially thaw a block if you want to cut it, and almost complete thawing is needed if you want to separate the fillets for rolling or some other special treatment. For quick thawing, put the unopened package in a deep dish and let cold water run over it. An hour should be long enough.

**To Broil Fish:** Broiling is an easy way to cook fresh or frozen steaks, fillets, or small whole fish. The broiler should be preheated if it is electric. Position the oven rack so the fish is about three inches from the heat if the fish is fresh or the next level down if frozen. Put fish on a greased broiler rack in pan. Brush both sides with melted butter, margarine, or oil. Put pan under hot broiler and cook fish until browned. Sprinkle lightly with salt and pepper and turn, broiling until browned. If steaks or fillets are very thin, turning is not necessary. Fish is cooked through when browned on first side.

**To Bake Fish:** Whole fish or large pieces are often baked. Cut off head and tail if necessary, salt inside lightly, and stuff loosely with bread or rice stuffing or simply lay slices of lemon, onion, celery leaves, parsley, dill, or other fresh herbs inside. Tie closed if stuffed, then put in a greased baking dish. Brush with oil or melted butter or margarine and bake at 450°F following the 10-Minute Rule for time.

**To Oven-Steam Fish:** This method is good for steaks or fillets. Put fish on greased heavy-duty foil, sprinkle lightly with salt and pepper, and add a slice of lemon and a sprinkling of dill, parsley, basil, marjoram, oregano, savory, or tarragon. Measure thickness of fish and wrap it securely in foil, sealing well. Put in baking dish and cook in 450°F oven 15 minutes total cooking time per inch of thickness or 30 minutes if frozen. Extra time is allowed over the usual 10-Minute Rule because the foil acts as an insulator.

**To Steam Fish on Top of Stove:** Set fish on a piece of greased heavy-duty foil and turn the foil up around the fish to form a dish, leaving the top open. Dot fish with butter or margarine and set the foil dish in a large pan of simmering water. Have the water rather shallow (about one-half inch) so it doesn't bubble into the foil. Cover the pan and simmer, using the 10-Minute Rule for time. Save the liquid in the foil and add it to an egg sauce or any other sauce you prefer for fish.

**To Poach Fish:** Whole fish or large pieces may be poached, usually to serve cold or to use for salads, casseroles, fish cakes, etc. Choose a pan large enough to hold the fish (a small fish poacher is useful for a small whole fish), salt the inside of the fish lightly, and set on a piece of dampened parchment paper or several thicknesses of cheesecloth. Add chopped onion, celery, lemon slices, herbs, etc., then wrap and tie securely. Measure thickness. Simmer, covered, in a mixture of white wine and water (or water alone) to cover, using the 10-Minute Rule for time, starting the timing at the point the liquid returns to simmering after adding fish.

## MEAT

Of course, unless you are a vegetarian, many meals are planned around meat. Meat certainly has its place in a nutritious meal since it supplies protein of the highest quality and it is a good source of the B vitamins and minerals. You've no doubt heard that, according to nutritionists, we have all been eating too much red meat and, in fact, I think most of us would find trouble eating the enormous steaks we perhaps once did. But reasonable servings of red meat, supplemented during the week with some fish or chicken, makes for satisfying as well as delicious eating.

Supermarkets now seem to be more conscious of the needs of the single person and twosomes, and packages of meat are often made up in small portions. If you can't find what you want, most supermarkets have a butcher available to cut what you request. I look for two small steaks or two pork chops in a package so I can have one for dinner that night and pop the second in the freezer for another day. It's often more economical to buy a very lean cut of meat rather than a piece that, though less expensive, is full of bone, fat and gristle.

Plan to use your meat as soon as possible after purchase. When you get it home, unwrap it, then put it on a plate and cover it loosely with waxed paper. Roasts and chops are safe in the refrigerator for two or three days, but ground meat should be used within two days. Don't freeze meat in the packages you get at the supermarket. Put it in freezer bags or wrap in foil.

**Cooking Meat:** Meat can be roasted, pan fried, broiled, pot roasted, braised, cooked in a stew, boiled, or barbecued.

**To Roast:** This is a dry heat method used for cooking tender cuts. For this method, use a 325°F oven. Put the roast in a roasting pan, fat side up, and cook, uncovered, and without liquid. A meat thermometer is a useful gadget if you intend to cook roasts fairly often.

**To Pan Fry:** This method is used for thin, tender cuts such as veal cutlets. Brown the meat on both sides in a small amount of fat, then cook more slowly, uncovered, until done.

**To Broil:** Broiling is often used for steaks and chops. The broiler should be preheated if the oven is electric. (Leave the door ajar during heating and broiling so unit does not shut off.) Put the meat on the rack in a broiler pan and place it a few inches under the heat source to brown on both sides. Cook to desired doneness.

**To Pot Roast:** This method is used for less tender roasts such as blade, cross rib, or shoulder. Brown the meat on all sides in a small amount of fat in a heavy pot or Dutch oven. Add a small amount of liquid (water, stock, tomato juice, leftover coffee, etc.), cover the pan tightly, and cook the meat slowly until tender, several hours.

**To Braise:** Less tender cuts, such as round steak, are braised. Brown the meat on both sides in a skillet in a little fat (you can dredge it first in seasoned flour), add liquid, cover the pan, and simmer until the meat is tender.

**To Stew:** Stewing is usually used for small pieces of less tender cuts, and vegetables are often added. In a large pan, brown the meat well in a little fat, then add seasoning and liquid. Cover the pan tightly and simmer until tender. If desired, add vegetables part way through cooking.

**To Boil:** This method is used for things like boiled dinner, brisket, cottage roll, corned beef, etc. Cover the meat with seasoned hot liquid and simmer until tender.

**To Barbecue:** Barbecues are so sophisticated today that you need the directions for the particular one you have. I hope that you, like me, still want to barbecue just for the wonderful taste. I have a small charcoal burner that cooks my one small steak, chop, or lamb patty to perfection.

## Beef

While you may not cook many good-sized roasts, occasionally you may want to serve one to company, so you will need some general information on cooking times for oven roasts, pot roasts, and steaks.

## COOKING TIMES FOR BEEF

### Roasting

Roast at 325°F for tender cuts such as standing or rolled rib. You may want to use a meat thermometer to measure internal temperature.

|  | Rare | Medium | Well done |
|---|---|---|---|
| Internal temperature: | 130° to 140° | 140° to 150° | 150° to 170° |
| Minutes per pound: | 20 to 25 | 25 to 30 | 30 to 35 |

### Pan Frying and Broiling

Pan fry and broil tender steaks such as sirloin and T-bone.

| Minutes per side for 1-inch steak: | | |
|---|---|---|
|  | Pan Frying | Broiling |
| Rare | 3 to 4 | 5 to 7 |
| Medium | 4 to 5 | 7 to 9 |
| Well-done | 5 to 6 | 9 to 11 |

## Pot Roasting

Use the pot roast method for less tender cuts such as blade, short or cross rib.

Always cooked to well done at least 30 minutes per pound.

## Veal

Veal is mild flavored, and milk-fed veal is very light pink in color. Although it comes from young animals, veal needs long, slow cooking (except for cutlets) to make it tender and develop its flavor. It has much less fat than other meats so it usually needs added fat for cooking.

Veal roasts are usually cooked until very tender and no trace of pink is left. The internal temperature should be 180°F and the time will range from about 40 to 50 minutes per pound. To pan fry chops or steaks, 1-inch thick, allow 20 minutes per side. Cutlets, pounded to one-quarter-inch thick, will take about 10 minutes. To broil chops in preheated broiler, brush lightly with oil and put 6 inches below the heat source. Allow about 12 minutes a side for 1-inch chops. To braise chops or steaks 1-inch thick, allow about 25 minutes a side.

## Pork

Some people still think of pork as a fat meat that is hard to digest, but today's pork is leaner and contains about the same number of calories in the cooked lean portions as those found in the lean of other meats. Today's pork can also be roasted to a lower internal temperature, so the roasts are more flavorful and juicier. Most cuts of pork are tender enough to be cooked by dry heat: pan frying, broiling, roasting, and barbecuing. Roasts should be cooked at 325 °F to 170 °F internal temperature and roasting times range from 30 to 40 minutes per pound. Chops 1-inch thick take about 25 minutes total broiling time (3 to 5 inches from heat source). To pan fry, allow 8 to 10 minutes per side and to braise allow about 30 minutes a side.

## Lamb

Whether domestic or imported, lamb is a tender, delicious meat that adds fine variety to meals. Lamb marked "spring lamb" comes from very young animals, while meat marked just "lamb" can come from animals as old as 14 months. Since lamb is a young animal, most of it is very tender and doesn't require long cooking. For medium doneness, roast a leg of lamb at 325 °F for 25 to 30 minutes per pound or until the meat thermometer registers 160 °F. For well done meat, cook 30 to 35 minutes per pound or until the meat thermometer reads 170 °F. To broil chops or patties 1-inch thick, allow 12 to 16 minutes total cooking time. To pan fry chops 1-inch thick, allow 15 minutes.

## Variety meats

Each of these meats (liver, kidney, heart, tongue, sweetbreads, brains, and tripe) should be prepared in a special way. If you want to cook any of them, I suggest you find individual recipes. However, there are some general rules. All liver can be pan fried; calf and baby beef liver broil well; beef and pork liver are good braised in tomato juice. Veal, lamb, and pork kidney can be pan fried or broiled while beef and pork kidney (sliced) are good braised. Heart is usually stuffed and baked. Tongue from beef, veal, pork, or lamb needs long, slow cooking in liquid. Sweetbreads come from the thymus gland of young beef and calves and require special treatment (membranes removed) before pan frying or boiling. Brains are treated in much the same way as sweetbreads. Tripe is the inner lining of the stomach of beef or sheep and is sold partially cooked, but since it is tough it needs long cooking once you get it home.

## PASTA

Pasta products (e.g., macaroni, spaghetti, noodles) are a source of some protein and have very little fat. Some pasta products available are made with high protein flour such as soya. In any case, it's hard to resist a plate of good spaghetti or macaroni and cheese, and pasta is one of the cereal choices from the four essential food groups required each day. Two ounces of pasta (one cup cooked) has less than 200 calories and when combined with protein foods such as lean meat, cheese, milk, or eggs you've got yourself a satisfying and nutritious dish.

Remember that macaroni and spaghetti double in volume when cooked, but noodles remain the same. To cook enough macaroni or spaghetti for two, heat five cups salted water to boiling in a large saucepan. (For larger amounts of pasta increase the amount of water.) Add a dollop of oil to keep the water from boiling over (a scant tablespoonful is plenty), then add one cup of pasta. Boil hard, uncovered, stirring occasionally to avoid sticking, until just tender but still slightly chewy. This takes about seven minutes. Drain and serve immediately for hot dishes or rinse with cold running water if pasta is to be used for a salad.

If you are cooking spaghetti whole, put one end in the boiling water and gradually curl it around the saucepan as it softens. Of course you can break it into pieces if you prefer.

## PASTRY

Perhaps you'll never want to make pastry, but since it is used for so many different things, it is useful to learn the basic techniques and what equipment is helpful.

You will need a good rolling pin, and a pastry blender is also good to have. Almost indispensable, especially to the novice, is a pastry cloth and sock for the rolling pin. They take most of the worry out of rolling pastry thin. You can find these things in the housewares department of most stores.

Only a few ingredients are needed for pastry. Flour for pastry may be all-purpose or cake and pastry. I prefer all-purpose, but either works well. The fat you use may be lard (which is animal fat) or vegetable shortening, and some cooks like to add a little butter for flavor. Lard makes the most tender and flaky pastry but, if you wish to avoid animal fat, vegetable shortening in a slightly larger quantity is fine.

A basic pastry recipe is provided on page 229. Don't be discouraged if your pastry isn't just right the first time. "Practice makes perfect" applies to nothing so much as to pastry making.

## POULTRY

Poultry is a good source of high quality protein and is rich in minerals and vitamins. The skin contains a lot of fat, so if you are watching your diet, don't eat it. Many chicken recipes now suggest skinning pieces before cooking.

Chicken and turkey may be bought whole or in various pieces, either fresh or frozen. Young chickens (broiler-fryers) up to four pounds can be roasted whole or cut up and broiled, baked, fried, or barbecued. Larger chickens, four pounds and over, are nearly always roasted. Capons of six to eight pounds are too large for most of us unless the whole family is coming to dinner! If you can find it, a fowl (older bird) is wonderful for stewed chicken and chicken stock. While cut-up chicken is more expensive than whole, it's a worthwhile expenditure for the convenience.

Cornish hens can be very useful. I find one hen is too much for me; I think you can count on each hen serving two. One hen usually weighs about one pound. It can be roasted or cut in half and broiled.

## ROASTING TIMETABLE FOR POULTRY

(For unstuffed birds; add one-half hour for stuffed.)

|  |  | Temp. | Approx. Time |
|---|---|---|---|
| **Chicken** | 2½ lb. | 375°F | 1½ hours |
|  | 4 lb. | 375°F | 2¼ hours |
| **Duck** | 3½ lb. | 350°F | 2 hours |

To roast chicken or duck, simply put the bird, breast side up, on a rack in a shallow roasting pan, rub all over with butter or margarine and roast, without a lid, basting occasionally, following the timetable above.

If you are roasting chicken without stuffing, you can put some celery leaves, an onion half, salt and pepper and perhaps some thyme and parsley inside to improve the flavor of the meat. I like to cover chicken loosely with foil for the first part of the cooking, then uncover it to let it brown well.

Turkey parts are also good and useful. They are usually baked or roasted. And a young duck is a nice change and makes three or four servings. I usually make a little duck pie with the leftovers.

Don't waste the giblets. Put them (minus the liver) in water to cover. Add a little salt, a few peppercorns, a bay leaf, a small piece of onion, some celery leaves and a generous sprig of parsley if you have it. Simmer until tender, adding liver for last five minutes if desired. Drain, saving liquid, and chop meat to add to gravy or stuffing. Use liquid for gravy or for recipes calling for chicken stock.

## RICE

Rice is limited in protein, but it contains all the essential amino acids (although some are in small quantities), and it is a source of iron and B-complex vitamins. As well, it is low in fat and cholesterol, gluten-free, low in sodium, and non-allergenic so it suits most special diets. Besides all that, it tastes good, has a nice texture, and adds interest to many dishes.

The most common types of rice are these:

**Regular white milled rice** can be short or long grain. One cup of this rice makes three cups cooked.

**Parboiled rice** is treated specially to save much of the natural vitamin and mineral content. It takes longer to cook than regular rice, and one cup makes three to four cups cooked.

**Pre-cooked rice** is ideal for hurry-up meals because it is cooked and dehydrated so it needs no more than the addition of liquid and a few minutes standing time. One cup yields one to two cups prepared.

**Brown rice** is the unpolished grain with the outer hull and only a small part of the bran removed. It has a special nutty flavor and requires more liquid and cooking time than regular rice. It also has more calories but more protein, minerals, niacin, and vitamin E too. It has a shorter shelf life than regular rice, so it should be refrigerated. One cup yields three to four cups cooked.

**Wild rice** is not really rice at all. It is the seed of a grass and is a great delicacy. One cup gives you three to four cups cooked. It requires special cooking so check the package for directions.

## TO COOK RICE FOR TWO

| | |
|---|---|
| ½ cup | uncooked rice (regular, parboiled, or brown) |
| 1 cup | liquid for regular rice<br>1¼ cups for parboiled or brown |
| ½ tsp. salt | |

Combine ingredients in a medium saucepan. Bring to a boil, stirring with a fork once or twice. Turn heat to low and cover pan tightly. Cook over low heat 15 minutes for regular rice, 20 to 25 minutes for parboiled rice, 45 minutes for brown rice. Do not lift lid during cooking. If rice is not quite tender or liquid is not absorbed, replace lid and cook 2 to 4 minutes longer.

## SALADS

Green leafy vegetables, with their vitamins and minerals, are essential to a healthful diet and there is no nicer way to eat them than in a good salad.

Tossed green salads are the simplest and most popular; try to use a variety of greens. When you are alone or just a couple, it's more difficult to keep a choice of greens, but I find if I plan to have a salad every day, I can do it. I wash my greens under cold running water (don't let them soak), dry them as well as possible either in a spinner or by tossing them lightly in a dish towel, then put them in a plastic bag wrapped loosely in dry dish towels or paper towels. Refrigerated until needed, they remain perfectly crisp and delicious. Greens should be torn rather than cut. Greens include a variety of lettuce types (iceberg, romaine, chicory, leaf, Boston, Bibb, butterhead) as well as spinach, parsley, and watercress.

Of course a salad can be its best only if the dressing is good too. And good dressings need the best ingredients possible. Olive oil gives its own delicate taste but a really good quality is needed, which can be quite expensive. Vegetable oil is acceptable. Wine vinegar gives a salad a tangy flavor, and fresh garlic and black pepper from a pepper mill help make salads special. A recipe for a basic **Tossed Green Salad** is on page 130.

Mixed vegetable salads please the adventurous cook. All sorts of combinations can be tried including fresh mushrooms, green pepper, pimento, zucchini, cucumber, radishes, raw cauliflower or broccoli, or even leftover cooked vegetables. A simple French dressing is good with these. You'll find a recipe for **Basic French Dressing** on page 141.

Potato, seafood and pasta salads are usually dressed with mayonnaise. An easy homemade mayonnaise is **Blender Mayonnaise** on page 144. Several companies are now making a "light" mayonnaise that is good.

For cabbage salad, you can use any cooked salad dressing or mayonnaise. Some slaws, such as the **Coleslaw** on page 138 have their own special dressing.

And for fruit salads or salads made with leaf lettuce, **Sweet Boiled Dressing** (my Mother's recipe) on page 143 is my favorite.

# SOUPS

Don't let anyone tell you that making stock is difficult. If you love homemade soup you'll find the stock making a pleasure. My favorite stocks are made from an assortment of raw or leftover meat, roast or steak bones, or from chicken or turkey bones and giblets. I save almost everything in the freezer, and when the bag of bones and scraps is full to overflowing and is taking up too much room, I brew up a big pot of stock. I like this kind of stock because the flavor varies a little each time depending on the scraps added, what vegetables are available, and what seasonings I use.

The richest stocks include some meat and a proportion of half bones and half meat is best of all. And, of course, fresh soup bones or chicken backs make wonderful stocks. Ham and lamb bones should be kept separate and when there are enough you can make a good ham stock for pea soup or lamb stock for barley soup. Pork bones tend to make the stock "sweet" so I don't save them.

If you plan to make stocks, you will need to invest in a large kettle, at least eight quarts in size (or you can make small amounts in a large saucepan or Dutch oven), and you will need to have freezer space to store the stock until you need it. A recipe for **Basic Soup Stock** is on page 64.

The great convenience of soup stock is that a good hearty soup can always be on the menu. Thaw the stock enough to get it out of the container if frozen and bring it to a boil. Then start adding vegetables — any vegetables you have in your refrigerator and any leftover meat too. Add the vegetables needing the longest cooking first (like potatoes and turnips), and work up through sliced carrots and celery and finally add leafy vegetables for the last minute or two. Add seasonings early in the cooking so they can simmer and develop their flavor.

Of course not all soups need a meat stock base. Chowders, like the **Corn Chowder** on page 67, and soups with vegetable base such as tomato juice are quick and good.

## VEGETABLES

Most of us are concerned about calories, cholesterol, salt, and sugar, and we are nearly all trying to improve our eating habits, so vegetables with their supply of vitamins and minerals have become, more than ever, an important part of meals. Vegetables provide a lot of variety, not only in taste, but in color and texture too. Luckily, most supermarkets now leave vegetables in bins and sell them by weight, so you can buy a few beans or peas, one or two tomatoes, or even a small cauliflower or broccoli. This way you can have an assortment of vegetables that can be used before they spoil. Of course, when you buy fresh vegetables, it's best to use them up quickly, but in the meantime, store them in the refrigerator — in the crisper if possible. Frozen vegetables should be kept frozen until used; canned vegetables should be stored in a cool place and dried peas, beans, etc. should be kept dry.

The main thing to learn about cooking vegetables is not to overcook. Not only does overcooking spoil the taste, but the color can be ruined and the nutrients lost.

Vegetables are cooked by these methods: baking, simmering, steaming, stir frying, butter steaming, pan frying, and microwaving. Cooked vegetables may be creamed, scalloped, or served au gratin.

**To Bake:** This is a good method for frozen vegetables. They can be put frozen in a casserole with a little butter or margarine and seasonings, then covered tightly and baked until tender at 350°F for about 30 minutes. Potatoes and squash are two other vegetables that are often baked.

**To Simmer:** Almost all vegetables can be cooked by this method. (Exceptions include potatoes, beets, and corn which should be covered with water and boiled.) For simmering, cook the vegetables gently in a small amount of boiling salted water until tender-crisp. There should be practically no water left when the vegetables are done. Add a little butter and salt and pepper plus a favorite herb and serve immediately.

**To Steam:** The little metal folding steamers are available everywhere, and they are the best thing that has happened to vegetables in years. Steamed vegetables should be deliciously tender and crisp. The water should be about one-half inch deep under the steamer (not touching the bottom of the steamer). Put the vegetables in the steamer over the boiling water and cover the pan tightly. After steaming, lift the steamer and vegetables out, drain the water from the pan, turn the vegetables into the pan, and add butter and seasonings.

**To Stir Fry:** For this method you can use a wok or a large heavy skillet. Add a little oil to the pan that has been heated to very hot. Add vegetables and toss, cooking as quickly as possible, until tender-crisp.

**To Butter Steam:** Butter steaming works well with summer squash, such as zucchini, and snow peas. Put a little butter or margarine and a small amount of water in a good-sized skillet along with the vegetable. Cover it tightly and cook for a short time, stirring a couple of times. Cook just until the vegetable is tender and the liquid is cooked away.

**To Pan Fry:** This method is usually used for eggplant and sometimes for ripe or green tomato slices.

Coat the vegetables with crumbs and fry in butter, margarine, or oil until brown on both sides.

**To Microwave:** I find that most vegetables can be steamed almost as quickly as the microwave cooks them, so I use my steamer more often. However, microwaved vegetables are very good. The book that came with your oven should give you the best instructions for each vegetable, but the general rule is to put the vegetables with a little water in a casserole or other dish that is microwave safe, cover, and cook at high the suggested time, stirring half way through cooking. Let stand, covered, two minutes, then serve.

A chart of cooking times for the most common vegetables is provided on page 145.

# RECIPES

Here are recipes I hope will appeal to you and inspire you to keep on cooking. There are simple ones, marked with this symbol ❦, ones that are a little harder, marked with this ❦❦, and ones that offer a bit of a challenge, marked this way ❦❦❦. The symbols don't mean so much the degree of expertise needed as the number of steps and time involved.

While most of the recipes are marked "Serves 2," a few say "Serves 4" and still others indicate "Makes 4 servings." Where I have said "Makes 4 servings," I am suggesting that the dish will be good for another meal, for example **Steak Soup** on page 72 which only gets better as it stands for a day or two and is great for lunch a second time. Where I have indicated "Serves 4" (and in the odd case "Serves 3") it means it's best to use the dish immediately and so to serve it when you have more than two for a meal.

When you plan your own menus, keep in mind the essential foods you need. I'm sure you know how important it is to eat a variety of foods every day and some from each of the four food groups listed in Canada's Food Guide. But — do you do it? Remember: You want to go on feeling well, and good food habits (as well as exercise) are a key to good health and energy.

**Meat and Alternates** is one of the food groups. This group includes meat, fish, poultry, dried beans, peas or lentils, nuts, seeds, cheese, and eggs. You need two servings a day; examples of servings are two to three ounces of meat, fish, or poultry; or one cup cooked dried beans, peas, lentils; or two ounces of cheddar or process cheese.

**Fruits and Vegetables** is my favorite food group. The Food Guide recommends four to five servings of these good things with at least two of the servings being vegetables. All fruit or vegetables, cooked or raw, and their juices are fine. Be sure to include yellow and green vegetables as well as salad greens. Examples of servings are one-half cup of any fruit, vegetable or juice, or one medium potato, tomato, peach, apple, orange, or banana.

**Breads and Cereals** are needed each day too. This group includes pasta, rice, cereals (both cooked and ready-to-eat), and bread (preferably whole grain). You need three to five servings of breads and cereals each day. Examples of servings are one slice of bread, one-half cup cooked cereal, three-quarters cup ready-to-eat cereal, one muffin, or one-half to three-quarters cup cooked rice, macaroni, or noodles.

**Milk and Milk Products** is the other essential group of foods. Included in this group are skim, 2%, or whole milk, buttermilk, yogurt, cottage cheese, cheddar cheese, process cheese, etc. You need two servings of these every day. Examples of servings are one cup milk, one cup yogurt, and one and a half ounces cheddar cheese.

# APPETIZERS, SNACKS, AND SIPS

# APPETIZERS, SNACKS, AND SIPS

No one really expects hors d'oeuvres and snacks to supply a great deal of the nutrients you need each day. However, that's no excuse for eating junk food. Remember you want to avoid fat and salt — so stay away from the salted peanuts and potato chips, please! On the other hand, for those who love to snack while watching TV, popcorn is a good candidate — providing you add no (or only a tiny bit) butter and salt. Popcorn is really satisfying for those who like something crunchy, and it provides fiber too.

You can add good things to the snack tray by using raw fruits and vegetables, rather than salty crackers, with spreads and dips. And there are recipes here for a few crackers I like to make because I find them tasty and inexpensive too.

You may like to serve a soup to start a special meal, but sometimes it's nice to have a different appetizer. For example, once in a while I like to go all out and serve a seafood cocktail or my very favorite **Curried Scallops** (page 53). These aren't inexpensive, of course, but they make that very special dinner party even more special.

The recipes for drinks include coolers for hot summer days and warmers for cold winter nights, as well as my favorite emergency breakfast.

# MUSHROOM CAVIAR 🐛

| | |
|---|---|
| 2 tbsp. | butter or margarine |
| ½ cup | green onions with tops, chopped very finely |
| ½ lb. | fresh mushrooms, chopped very finely |
| 2 tbsp. | lemon juice |
| ¼ tsp. | salt |
| | Freshly ground pepper |
| ½ tsp. | Worcestershire sauce |
| Dash | Tabasco |
| ⅓ cup | light mayonnaise |
| | Melba toast or crackers |

Heat butter or margarine in skillet. Add onions and cook quickly, stirring, 1 minute. Add mushrooms and cook and stir until mixture is golden and quite dry. Remove from heat, turn into bowl, and cool. Add remaining ingredients except melba toast or crackers, blend well and taste, adjusting seasoning if necessary. Chill well and serve as a spread with toast or crackers.

Makes about 1 cup.

## GINGER-NUT SPREAD ❦

| ⅓ cup | hazelnuts (filberts) |
| 250 g pkg. | cream cheese at room temperature |
| ¼ cup | finely chopped preserved ginger |
| 1 tbsp. | lemon juice |
| | Whole wheat or sesame crackers |

Heat oven to 350 °F. Put hazelnuts in a shallow pan and toast in oven 10 minutes, shaking pan often. Cool and chop finely.

Mix all ingredients well, except crackers, pack in a small bowl, cover, and refrigerate several hours. Bring to room temperature before serving as a spread with crackers.

Makes about 1¼ cups.

## CREAMY CHUTNEY SPREAD ❦

| 125 g pkg. | cream cheese at room temperature |
| 1 tbsp. | thick liquid from commercial chutney |
| ¼ tsp. | curry powder |
| 2 tbsp. | finely chopped walnuts |

Combine cheese, chutney liquid, and curry powder. Mix well. Pack into a small bowl and sprinkle with walnuts. Cover and chill. Serve with crackers, apple slices, or raw vegetables.

Makes about ½ cup.

## CHEESE SPREAD ✿

| | |
|---|---|
| 1 cup | low-fat cottage cheese |
| 1 cup | grated old cheddar cheese |
| 1 tbsp. | finely chopped green onion |
| 1 tbsp. | chopped parsley |
| ½ cup | finely chopped celery |
| ¼ cup | toasted sesame seeds |
| ¼ tsp | salt |
| | Fresh ground black pepper |
| 1 tbsp. | mayonnaise |

Mash cottage cheese with a fork until as smooth as possible. Stir in remaining ingredients. Use as a spread on crackers or for sandwiches.

Makes 2 cups.

## CHEESE NIBBLE WAFERS 🌾

| | |
|---|---|
| 1 ½ cups | sifted all-purpose flour |
| ½ tsp. | salt |
| 1 tbsp. | finely chopped chives |
| ½ cup | soft butter or margarine |
| ½ lb. | process cheese, grated (about 2½ cups) |

Heat oven to 350 °F. Grease cookie sheets.

Sift flour and salt into a bowl. Add chives and toss with a fork. Cream butter or margarine and cheese together until well blended. Blend in flour mixture. Shape dough into small balls about 1 inch in diameter, put on cookie sheets and flatten each ball to a little less than ¼-inch thick by pressing with the floured tines of a fork. Prick top of each round in several places.

Bake 12 to 15 minutes or until lightly browned.

Makes about 3½ dozen.

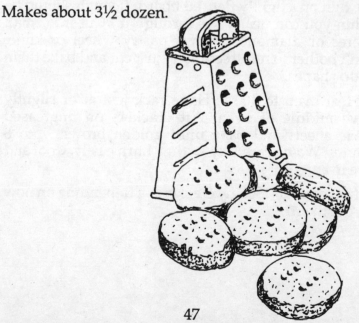

# HEALTH CRACKERS ❧ ❧

| | |
|---|---|
| 1 cup | whole wheat flour |
| ¼ cup | soy flour |
| ¼ cup | sesame seeds (hulled or unhulled) |
| 2 tbsp. | wheat germ |
| 2 tbsp. | chopped sunflower seeds |
| ¼ tsp. | salt |
| 2 tbsp. | vegetable oil |
| ⅓ to ½ cup | cold water |

Mix first 6 ingredients in a medium bowl. Add oil and blend well with a fork. Add ¼ cup of the water, mixing well, then add more water, 1 tbsp. at a time, to make a firm dough that sticks together and rolls easily. Knead on a floured board for 10 minutes.

Pull off small chunks of dough and roll each chunk very thin on a lightly floured board. (Dough should be so thin you can nearly see through it.) Cut into small squares or diamonds with a pastry wheel or knife. (Don't bother to reroll scraps — just cut and bake them in odd shapes.)

Heat oven to 400°F. Have rack just at or slightly above middle of oven. Put crackers on ungreased cookie sheets and bake until golden brown, 7 to 8 minutes. Watch carefully — they burn easily. Cool and store in a tightly sealed tin.

Makes up to 150 tiny crackers — depending on how you cut them.

## POTATO WAFERS 🍎

| | |
|---|---|
| 1 cup | riced boiled potatoes |
| ½ cup | soft butter or margarine |
| 1 cup | sifted all-purpose flour |
| 1 | egg, lightly beaten |
| 1 | egg yolk |
| 2 tsp. | milk |
| | Salt |
| | Caraway seeds |

Blend first 4 ingredients together well with a fork to make a smooth dough. Chill 30 minutes.

Heat oven to 400°F. Grease cookie sheets.

Roll dough very thin (about 1/16 inch) on a floured board. Cut into 3 x 1-inch strips and put on prepared cookie sheets. Beat egg yolk and milk together lightly with a fork. Brush tops of strips of dough with this mixture. Sprinkle lightly with salt and generously with caraway seeds. Bake about 12 minutes or until lightly browned.

Makes about 36.

## CHICKEN LIVER PATE 🦃 🦃

| | |
|---|---|
| ½ lb. | chicken livers |
| 2 tbsp. | butter or margarine |
| ½ | small clove garlic, minced |
| Dash | salt |
| Dash | pepper |
| 1½ tbsp. | brandy |
| ½ pkg.<br>(125 g) | cream cheese at room temperature |
| 1 tbsp. | mayonnaise |
| 1½ tsp. | Worcestershire sauce |
| ½ tsp. | lemon juice |
| ¼ tsp. | salt |
| Dash | pepper |
| ⅛ tsp. | curry powder |
| Dash | nutmeg |
| Dash | cayenne |
| ¼ cup | toasted sesame seeds |
| | French bread or crackers |

Wash and dry chicken livers. Trim and cut into pieces. Heat butter or margarine in skillet and cook livers and garlic, stirring constantly, until livers are lightly browned but still pink inside (3 to 4 minutes). Sprinkle with dash salt and pepper. Remove from heat.

Lift livers out of pan with a slotted spoon and set aside. Add brandy to pan and stir to scrape up all browned bits. Pour brandy and drippings into the blender. Cut up cream cheese and add to blender along with mayonnaise, Worcestershire sauce, lemon juice, ¼ tsp. salt, dash pepper, curry powder, nutmeg, and cayenne. Blend until mixture is smooth.

Add chicken livers a few at a time, blending until smooth after each addition. Refrigerate several hours.

Stir sesame seeds into pâté shortly before serving and pack into a small crock or bowl. Serve with French bread or crackers.

Makes about 1 cup.

## SEAFOOD COCKTAIL SAUCE 🦐

| ½ cup | commercial chili sauce |
| ⅓ cup | ketchup |
| 3 tbsp. | prepared horseradish |
| 2 tbsp. | lemon juice |
| 1½ tsp. | Worcestershire sauce |
| Dash | Tabasco |
| Dash | black pepper |

Combine all ingredients and chill. Use for any type of seafood cocktail.

Makes about 1 cup.

**Note:** This is quite hot. If you prefer it milder, reduce the amount of horseradish and omit the Tabasco.

## AVOCADO-CRAB COCKTAIL ❦

| | |
|---|---|
| | Shredded lettuce |
| 1 | small avocado, peeled and cubed |
| 5-oz. can | crab, drained and flaked |
| 1½ tsp. | grated onion |
| ¼ cup | light mayonnaise |
| 1½ tsp. | chili sauce |
| 1½ tsp. | finely chopped chutney |
| 4 small wedges | avocado (optional) |

Line bottom of 4 sherbet glasses with shredded lettuce shortly before serving time. Combine avocado cubes, crab, and onion, tossing lightly with a fork. Divide mixture among prepared glasses. Blend mayonnaise, chili sauce, and chutney and spoon some of mixture over each cocktail. Top each with a wedge of avocado and serve immediately.

Serves 4.

## CURRIED SCALLOPS ✿

| | |
|---|---|
| 1 lb. | fresh or frozen scallops |
| ¼ cup | fine, dry bread crumbs |
| ¼ tsp. | salt |
| 3 tbsp. | butter |
| 1 tsp. | curry powder |
| 2 tsp. | lemon juice |
| 4 thin slices | lemon |

Thaw scallops if frozen. Heat oven to 450°F. Butter 4 large scallop shells or shallow individual baking dishes. Rinse scallops under cold running water and dry well on paper towelling. Combine bread crumbs and salt in a flat dish and roll each scallop in the mixture to coat with crumbs on all sides. Divide scallops equally among the scallop shells or baking dishes, putting them in a single layer.

Melt butter in a small saucepan. Add curry powder and cook gently 2 minutes, stirring. Stir in lemon juice and drizzle this mixture over the scallops. Lay a lemon slice on top of each serving. Bake about 10 minutes or until scallops are tender. Serve immediately.

Serves 4 as an appetizer.

## PITA TRIANGLES ❦

| | |
|---|---|
| 1 round | whole wheat pita bread (about 6 inches in diameter) |
| | Butter or margarine |
| | Sesame seeds |
| | Grated cheese |

Split the pita into halves by cutting carefully around the edge with a sharp pointed knife; then cut each half into 8 triangles. Put them on a cookie sheet, inner side down, and slip under hot broiler to brown outside a little more, 1 or 2 minutes. Watch carefully so they don't burn.

Remove from oven and turn pieces, then spread lightly with butter or margarine and sprinkle half with sesame seeds, the other half with grated cheese (Parmesan is good). Slip back under broiler until bubbling and lightly browned, about 1 minute. Cool on rack and store in a tight tin. Good with soup or as a snack.

Makes 16 triangles.

## SPRITZER 🦌

For each drink, combine half chilled,  dry white wine and half chilled soda water in a tall glass or goblet. Add some ice cubes and a twist of lemon. For a rosé spritzer, substitute rosé wine (as dry as possible) for the dry white wine.

## KIR 🦌

For each drink, combine 3 or 4 oz. chilled, dry white wine with 1 oz. cassis (or make the combination to your taste) in a large wine glass or goblet for a beautiful, elegant, and refreshing drink. Add ice if desired.

   **Note:** Cassis is a black currant cordial available in liquor stores.

## PINK BANANA WHIP 🦌

| | |
|---|---|
| 1 cup | chilled cranberry-apple drink |
| 1 cup | chilled fresh orange juice |
| ½ | ripe banana |
| 4 | ice cubes |

Combine ingredients in blender and blend until well mixed. Pour into 2 tall glasses and serve immediately.

Serves 2.

## SANGRIA ❦ ❦

| | |
|---|---|
| ¼ cup | sugar |
| ½ cup | cold water |
| 1 | lime, sliced paper thin |
| 1 | orange, sliced paper thin |
| 1 | lemon, sliced paper thin |
| | Ice cubes |
| 1 bottle | dry, full-bodied red wine |

Combine sugar and water in a small saucepan and heat, stirring constantly, until sugar is dissolved and syrup is simmering. Remove from heat and add lime, orange, and lemon. Let fruit and syrup stand at room temperature several hours, stirring occasionally.

Pour fruit and syrup into a large pitcher. Add 1 tray of ice cubes and pour in the wine. Stir to blend and serve as a punch or as a beverage with a summer meal.

Makes about 5 cups.

**Note:** If you prefer a milder wine taste, add about half as much soda water as wine just before serving.

## MINTED ICED TEA ❦ ❦

| | |
|---|---|
| | Mint sprigs |
| 1 tbsp. | sugar |
| 2 | whole cloves |
| 2 cups | strong, freshly brewed tea |
| 2 tbsp. | lemon juice |
| | Soda water |

Put 6 mint sprigs and the sugar in a pitcher and crush with a wooden spoon. Add cloves and pour in the hot tea. Stir well.

Fill 2 tall glasses (about 12 oz.) ¾ full with crushed ice. Strain the hot tea over the ice, filling the glasses about ¾ full. Add 1 tbsp. lemon juice to each glass and fill with soda water. Garnish each glass with a sprig of mint.

Serves 2.

## GRAPEFRUIT CASSIS 🍷 🍷

| 2½ cups | grapefruit juice |
|---------|-------------------|
| ¼ cup | cassis syrup (black currant nectar) |
| | Chilled soda water |
| | Mint sprigs |

Freeze half of the grapefruit juice in an ice cube tray. Chill remaining juice.

For each serving, fill a tall (12 to 16 oz.) glass with frozen juice cubes. Combine the chilled juice and cassis syrup and pour about ⅔ cup into each glass. Fill with soda water and garnish with mint.

Serves 2.

**Note:** You can find cassis syrup, which is non-alcoholic, in supermarkets and specialty food stores.

## ORANGE EGGNOG 🐦

| 1 | egg |
| 1 tsp. | liquid honey |
| 3 tbsp. | frozen orange juice concentrate, thawed |
| ¼ tsp. | vanilla extract |
| 1 cup | skim milk |

Put egg, honey, orange juice concentrate, and vanilla in the glass of the blender and blend 15 seconds. Add milk and blend until smooth and foamy. Pour into a large glass and serve immediately.

Serves 1.

## EMERGENCY BREAKFAST DRINK 🐦

| ½ cup | skim milk |
| ½ cup | plain skim milk yogurt |

Fresh or drained canned fruit (1 small banana or 1 peach or ½ cup berries or ½ canned pear, etc.)

Put all ingredients in blender and blend until thick and foamy. Pour into a large glass and serve immediately.

Serves 1.

## COFFEE CONTINENTAL 🐾

| | |
|---|---|
| 1 cup | boiling water |
| 2 tbsp. | instant coffee |
| 1 cup | hot milk |
| 2 thin strips | lemon rind |
| | Sugar (optional) |

Pour water over coffee in china pot or pitcher. Stir, then stir in the hot milk. Rub rims of 2 coffee mugs with lemon peel and drop the strips into the cups. Pour in the hot coffee. Pass the sugar.

Serves 2.

**Note:** Cut lemon rind lengthwise through the yellow part of the rind only.

## TOE WARMER 🐾

| | |
|---|---|
| 19 oz. can | apple juice |
| 2 tbsp. | brown sugar |
| 3 | whole cloves |
| | Small cinnamon stick, broken |
| 1 slice | orange (unpeeled), cut in half |

Combine all ingredients except the orange slice in a saucepan. Bring to simmering, reduce heat, and continue heating without boiling, 20 minutes.

Put a half slice of orange in each of 2 large mugs. Strain the apple juice into the mugs.

Serves 2.

# COCOA ☕

| 1 tbsp. | cocoa |
| 1½ tsp. | sugar |
| 2 cups | milk |

Combine cocoa and sugar in a cup or small bowl. Add a little of the cold milk and stir until smooth. Heat remaining milk to scalding (small bubbles appear around the edge) in a small saucepan. Gradually stir some of the hot milk into the cocoa mixture until smooth, then stir the cocoa into the remaining hot milk. Heat gently (do not boil), stirring, 1 minute. Pour into cups or mugs.

Serves 2.

**Note:** Be sure to use pure cocoa — not the instant chocolate drink. This is not very sweet — it's the way I like it. You can add more sugar of course. I sometimes add about ¼ tsp. pure vanilla extract, which seems to accentuate the cocoa flavor.

# SOUPS AND
# SAUCES

# SOUPS AND SAUCES

It's hard to judge the nutritive value of a soup stock because, of course, it varies with the proportion of meat or vegetables to water, as well as with what vegetables are added. However, clear broth is delicious and gives the taste buds a wallop to stimulate appetite for the rest of the meal. If you add milk, rice, lentils, vegetables, or meat the soup can provide more than one of the essential foods you need each day.

While sauces aren't likely to add much to your daily nutrition, they do add variety to meals. Because they usually also add calories without the benefit of plenty of nutrients, most of them should be used for special occasions only.

## BASIC MEAT, CHICKEN, OR TURKEY STOCK

| | |
|---|---|
| 3 or 4 lb. | meat and bones |
| | Cold water |
| 1 | small onion, peeled |
| 1 | carrot |
| 2 | large stalks celery with leaves |
| 2 | leeks (optional) |
| 2 tsp. | salt |
| 1 | bay leaf |
| 4 large sprigs | parsley |
| ¼ tsp. | dried leaf thyme |
| 4 | peppercorns |

Put meat and bones into a large soup pot or kettle. Cover with cold water to about 2 inches above ingredients. Bring to a boil and skim off any scum that rises to the surface. Add coarsely cut up onion, carrot, celery, and leeks, and the seasonings. Reduce heat, cover and simmer very gently 4 to 5 hours or until you are sure all the goodness has been cooked out of the ingredients.

Set a sieve in a large bowl and pour the stock through the sieve. (Line the sieve with several thicknesses of cheesecloth if you want a clear stock, but it isn't necessary if you are using the stock for soups that have a lot of added ingredients.) Discard bones and vegetables. Keep scraps of meat to add back into soup if desired.

Taste the stock and, if it seems watery, return it to the pot and boil it, uncovered, until it cooks down and the flavor is good. Cool as quickly as possible by setting in ice water and then put in refrigerator until fat rises to the surface and hardens. Lift off fat and discard or freeze some chicken or turkey fat to replace butter in casseroles.

Use the stock immediately or pour it into large jars (leave 1 inch head space) or tight plastic containers and freeze.

Makes about 10 cups.

**Note:** If you want a brown stock with a stronger flavor, brown beef meat, bones, and vegetables in a roasting pan in a 450°F oven before putting them in the soup kettle.

## MUSHROOM CONSOMME 🐞

| | |
|---|---|
| 4 oz. | fresh mushrooms |
| 10-oz. can | beef consommé |
| 1 cup | water |
| | Pepper |
| 2 tbsp. | dry sherry |

Wash mushrooms, trim, and chop very finely. Bring consommé and water to a boil. Add mushrooms, lower heat, cover, and simmer 20 minutes. Add pepper to taste, stir in sherry, and serve.

Serves 2.

## CLEAR CELERY SOUP ❦ ❦

| | |
|---|---|
| 3 cups | homemade chicken stock (page 64) |
| 2 large stalks | celery (with leaves), chopped coarsely |
| 4 sprigs | parsley |
| | Salt and pepper (optional) |
| 1 tbsp. | chopped parsley |
| | Tiny Croutons (see below) |

Bring stock to a boil, add celery and sprigs of parsley, cover, and simmer about 30 minutes or until there is a very distinct taste of celery to the soup. Strain soup, taste, and add salt and pepper if needed. Sprinkle in chopped parsley. Ladle into soup bowls and top with **Tiny Croutons.**

Serves 2.

## TINY CROUTONS

| | |
|---|---|
| 1 tbsp. | butter or margarine |
| | Celery salt |
| ½ cup | small day-old bread cubes (less than ¼ inch) |

Heat butter or margarine in small heavy skillet. Add a shake of celery salt and bread cubes. Cook and stir over medium heat until bread is crisp and golden. Drain and cool on paper towelling.

# CORN CHOWDER 🐮 🐮

| | |
|---|---|
| 2 | medium potatoes |
| 1 tbsp. | margarine or cooking oil |
| ⅔ cup | chopped celery |
| 1 | small onion, chopped |
| 12-oz. can | whole kernel corn (or 1½ cups fresh cooked corn cut from cobs) |
| ½ tsp. | salt |
| ¼ tsp. | dried leaf basil |
| 2 tbsp. | chopped parsley |
| ⅛ tsp. | black pepper |
| 2 cups | skim milk |

Scrub potatoes and cook them in their jackets in boiling, salted water. Drain, saving cooking water. Peel and dice potatoes. Heat margarine or oil in a medium saucepan, add celery and onion, and cook gently 3 minutes, stirring constantly. Add corn, potato cubes, salt, basil, parsley, and pepper. Cover and heat gently 5 minutes, then stir in milk and 1 cup of the potato cooking water. (Add water to make up amount if necessary.) Heat gently until very hot, stirring often.

Makes 4 servings.

## BLENDER CUCUMBER-BEET SOUP 🐞🐞

| | |
|---|---|
| 1 | medium cucumber |
| ½ cup | coarsely cut up cooked beets (canned are fine) |
| 2 | green onions with tops, cut up coarsely |
| 1 large sprig | parsley. |
| 1 small bunch | celery leaves |
| ½ tsp. | salt |
| | Dash white pepper |
| 2 cups | buttermilk |
| | Cucumber slivers |

Peel cucumber, cut it in half lengthwise, and scrape out and discard seeds. Chop coarsely into a blender. Add remaining ingredients, except cucumber slivers, and blend until smooth. Chill very well, then serve topped with a few slivers of cucumber.

Makes 4 servings.

# GAZPACHO 🐛 🐛

| | |
|---|---|
| 1 clove | garlic, peeled and cut in half |
| 4 | medium tomatoes |
| ¼ cup | finely chopped peeled and seeded cucumber |
| ¼ cup | finely chopped green onion |
| ¼ tsp. | dried leaf oregano, crumbled or 1 tsp. finely snipped fresh basil leaves |
| 1 tbsp. | olive oil |
| 1½ tsp. | red wine vinegar |
| ½ tsp. | salt |
| | Fresh ground pepper |
| 2 | ice cubes |
| | Chopped parsley |
| 2 | lime slices (optional) |

Sprinkle a small amount of salt into a pottery bowl. Dip cut side of garlic in salt and rub it all over inside of bowl. Discard garlic.

Peel and seed tomatoes. Chop 2 tomatoes finely and blend the other 2 in the blender or press through a sieve to make a puree (about 1 cup). Combine all ingredients except ice cubes, parsley, and lime slices in the bowl. Cover and chill several hours.

Put an ice cube into each of 2 chilled soup bowls at serving time and ladle in the Gazpacho. Sprinkle with parsley and add a lime slice to each.

Serves 2.

## MULLIGATAWNY ✿ ✿

| | |
|---|---|
| 2 tbsp. | butter or margarine |
| ½ cup | chopped onion |
| 1 cup | chopped celery |
| 2 tsp. (or more) | curry powder |
| 1½ tbsp. | flour |
| 4 cups | homemade chicken stock (page 64) |
| ¼ cup | chopped, peeled tart apple |
| ½ cup | cooked rice |
| ½ cup | cooked chicken in thin strips |
| ½ tsp. | salt |
| ⅛ tsp. | pepper |
| Pinch | dried leaf thyme |
| ½ cup | hot, light cream |

Heat butter or margarine in medium saucepan. Add onion and celery, cook and stir 3 minutes over medium heat, then add curry powder and stir 2 minutes. Sprinkle in flour and stir to blend, then remove from heat and add chicken stock all at once, stirring to blend. Return to medium heat and stir until boiling, slightly thickened, and smooth. Turn down heat, cover, and simmer 30 minutes.

Add apple, rice, chicken, salt, pepper, and thyme and simmer 15 minutes. Stir in cream and heat, but do not boil. Serve immediately.

Makes 4 servings.

## SPICY TOMATO BOUILLON ❦

| | |
|---|---|
| 2 cups | tomato juice |
| ½ cup | water |
| Pinch | salt |
| 1 | beef bouillon cube (or 1 tsp. beef stock mix) |
| 3 | whole cloves |
| 2 | peppercorns |
| 2 small slices | onion |
| 1 strip | lemon peel, 1-inch long |
| ½ tsp. | Worcestershire sauce |
| Dash | Tabasco |
| Dash | nutmeg |
| 2 thin slices | lemon |

Heat tomato juice and water in a saucepan. Add salt and bouillon cube or beef stock mix and stir until dissolved. Add cloves, peppercorns, onion, and lemon rind, bring to a boil, cover, reduce heat, and simmer 10 minutes. Add Worcestershire sauce, Tabasco, and nutmeg and strain into soup cups or mugs. Top each serving with a lemon slice.

Serves 2.

## STEAK SOUP 🐾🐾🐾

| | |
|---|---|
| 1 tbsp. | butter or margarine |
| 1 tbsp. | cooking oil |
| 2 tbsp. | finely chopped onion |
| 1 lb. | round steak, trimmed and cut in ½-inch cubes |
| 1½ tbsp. | flour |
| 1½ tsp. | paprika |
| ½ tsp. | salt |
| ⅛ tsp. | pepper |
| 2 cups | beef stock (see page 64) |
| 1 cup | water |
| 1 | small bay leaf |
| 1 large sprig | celery leaves |
| 2 large sprigs | parsley |
| ¼ tsp. | dried leaf marjoram |
| ¾ cup | ¼-inch potato cubes |
| ¾ cup | ¼-inch carrot cubes |
| ¾ cup | ¼-inch celery cubes |
| 2 tbsp. | tomato paste |

Heat butter or margarine and oil in a saucepan over medium heat. Add onion and stir 5 minutes. Turn heat to high, add meat, and stir until well browned. Reduce heat to medium. Combine flour, paprika, salt, and pepper and sprinkle over meat. Stir to blend, then gradually stir in beef stock and water.

Tie bay leaf, celery leaves, and parsley together with string and add along with marjoram. Bring to a boil, turn heat to low, cover, and simmer 1 hour. Lift out and discard bunch of herbs. Add vegetables and simmer, partly covered, until vegetables are tender and soup is quite thick, about 1 hour. Add tomato paste and simmer, uncovered, until thick like stew, about 15 minutes. Taste and adjust seasoning.

Makes 4 servings.

## QUICK CORN SOUP ❦

| | |
|---|---|
| 10-oz. can | cream soup (chicken, mushroom, or celery) |
| ½ cup | low-fat plain yogurt |
| 10-oz. can | creamed corn |
| Pinch | anise seeds (optional) |

Combine ingredients and heat to just below the boiling point. Serve immediately.

Serves 2.

# FRESH TOMATO SAUCE 🐌 🐌

| | |
|---|---|
| 2 tbsp. | olive oil |
| 1½ cups | chopped onion |
| ½ cup | finely grated carrot |
| 1 clove | garlic, minced |
| 2 lb. (about 6 medium) | tomatoes, peeled and chopped |
| ½ cup | chicken stock |
| ½ tsp. | salt |
| ¼ tsp. | black pepper |
| ½ tsp. | dried leaf basil (use 2 tsp. chopped fresh if you can get it) |
| 2 tbsp. | minced parsley |

Heat oil in medium saucepan. Add onion and garlic and cook gently, stirring, 10 minutes. Add remaining ingredients, cover, and simmer 1½ hours.

Taste and adjust seasonings if necessary.

Use immediately or freeze to use over cooked pasta, spaghetti squash, steamed zucchini, or combine with chicken stock to make a delicious soup.

If you have a food processor, combine onion, carrot, and garlic and process until chopped finely. Cook them for 10 minutes in the olive oil. Process the tomatoes, fresh basil (if you use it), and parsley until chopped finely, add them, along with the remaining ingredients. Continue with the recipe as directed.

Makes about 3 cups sauce.

**Note:** To peel fresh tomatoes, dip them in boiling water, count to 12 and lift out. The skins will slip off easily. When good tomatoes are not available, you can replace the fresh tomatoes with a 28-oz. can of tomatoes.

## QUICK VEGETABLE CHOWDER ❦

| | |
|---|---|
| 1 cup | frozen mixed vegetables |
| ¼ cup | water |
| 10-oz. can | cream of celery soup |
| 1½ cups | skim or 2% milk |
| ¼ cup | grated cheddar cheese |
| 1 tbsp. | chopped parsley |

Put vegetables and water into a small saucepan, bring to a boil, reduce heat to medium, cover, and cook 3 minutes. Stir in soup and milk and heat gently, stirring often, until vegetables are just tender and soup is hot. Ladle into 2 bowls. Mix cheese and parsley and sprinkle some on each bowl of soup.

Serves 2.

# WHITE SAUCE 🐓

*Medium thickness*

| | |
|---|---|
| 2 tbsp. | butter or margarine |
| 2 tbsp. | flour |
| ¼ tsp. | salt |
| ⅛ tsp. | pepper |
| 1 cup | milk |

Melt butter or margarine in a small, heavy saucepan over medium heat. Sprinkle in flour, salt, and pepper and stir to blend. Remove from heat, add the milk all at once, and stir to blend. Return to heat and bring to a boil, stirring constantly. Reduce heat and stir 1 minute.

Makes 1 cup.

## VARIATIONS:

### Cheese Sauce

Add ¼ tsp. dry mustard with the seasonings and ½ cup grated old cheddar cheese at the end of cooking, stirring until cheese is melted.

### Curry Sauce

Add ½ tsp. curry powder to butter or margarine and cook gently 1 minute, stirring, before adding the flour and seasoning.

### Egg Sauce

Add 2 chopped, hard-cooked eggs to prepared sauce.

# HOLLANDAISE SAUCE 🍎 🍎

*For vegetables, fish, shellfish, poultry, and eggs*

| | |
|---|---|
| 1 | egg yolk |
| 1 tbsp. | lemon juice |
| ¼ cup | very cold butter |

Put butter in the freezer for a few minutes to be sure it is very cold.

Put egg yolk and lemon juice into a small, heavy saucepan and stir together with a wooden spoon. Add half the butter (keep remaining portion cold), set over very low heat and stir until butter melts. Add remaining butter and continue heating and stirring until butter melts and sauce thickens. Be sure to cook very slowly. It should not boil. Serve hot or at room temperature.

Makes ⅓ cup.

## TARTAR SAUCE 🐿

*For fish*

| | |
|---|---|
| ¼ cup | light mayonnaise |
| 1 tbsp. | finely chopped dill pickle |
| 1 small | green onion, finely chopped |
| 1½ tsp. | finely chopped parsley |
| 1 tsp. | chopped capers (optional) |
| 1 tsp. | finely chopped pimento |
| ⅛ tsp. | prepared mustard |
| ½ tsp. | lemon juice |

Mix all ingredients and let stand in the refrigerator 30 minutes to blend flavors.

Makes about ⅓ cup.

## QUICK SAUCE FOR VEGETABLES 🐿

| | |
|---|---|
| ½ cup | cream of celery soup |
| 2 tbsp. | light mayonnaise |
| 1½ tsp. | lemon juice |

Put ingredients into a small, heavy saucepan and stir over lowest heat just until warmed through.

Makes ½ cup. (Good over broccoli or asparagus.)

**Variation:** Heat 1 tsp. butter or margarine in small saucepan. Add ½ tsp. curry powder and stir over low heat 2 minutes, then stir in remaining ingredients and heat as directed above.

# QUICK MEAT LOAF SAUCE 🦂

| | |
|---|---|
| 1 tsp. | butter or margarine |
| 1 tbsp. | finely chopped green onion |
| ½ cup | cream of mushroom soup |
| ¼ cup | milk |
| ½ tsp. | Worcestershire sauce |
| Dash | Tabasco |
| ¼ cup | chopped dill pickles |

Heat butter or margarine in a small saucepan. Add onion and cook gently, stirring, 3 minutes. Add remaining ingredients and stir over low heat until hot but not boiling.

Makes ¾ cup.

# GRAVY ❧ ❧

*Probably none of us should have gravy — but it's irresistible! Just try to use as little of the fat as possible when making it.*

**Pan Gravy:** Remove meat from roasting pan and drain off almost all the fat (you'll be surprised how little you need). Leave all the brown bits in the pan. For 1 cup of gravy, sprinkle in 2 tbsp. flour and stir until lightly browned. Remove from heat and add 1 cup of hot liquid gradually, stirring constantly. You can use water or stock. Return to heat and bring to boiling, stirring up all the browned bits from the bottom of the pan. Simmer 2 minutes, season with salt and pepper. If you like a thinner gravy use a little less flour.

**Kettle Gravy:** This is the kind of gravy you make for pot roast. After meat is removed from the kettle or Dutch oven, pour the liquid in the pan into a deep bowl or a glass measuring cup. Let stand until fat rises to the surface (to speed this up add a few ice cubes), then skim off fat. Add enough water to the liquid remaining to make 2 cups, then return to kettle and heat to boiling. Shake 2 tbsp. flour with ¼ cup cold water in a small jar to blend well, then stir this mixture into the boiling liquid gradually. Boil, stirring, 2 minutes. Season with salt and pepper and a small sprinkling of nutmeg.

# MAIN DISHES

# MAIN DISHES

Main dishes supply us with the Meat and Alternates group of foods recommended by Canada's Food Guide. These foods are rich in protein (for tissue building and repair and building of antibodies to fight infection), B vitamins (for maintenance of healthy nervous system and digestive tract, healthy skin and eyes), and iron (which, with protein, forms hemoglobin, the part of blood that transports oxygen and carbon dioxide). Although animal protein foods do not contain much fiber, dried peas, beans, lentils, nuts, and seeds are good sources. They, however, do not contain all the essential amino acids (meats do) and so must be used along with animal protein or combined with other plant protein.

These recipes include only one roast, since most of you will probably seldom cook one. (If you need information about roasts, see the Meat section on pages 23 to 29.) However, since I do find I like to prepare a small pot roast occasionally, I hope you, too, will enjoy trying **Yankee Pot Roast.** There are also recipes using steaks, chops, ground meat, chicken, and several kinds of fish and eggs. And there is quite a nice choice of casseroles too, if, like most of us, you are fond of these lively mixtures.

## STEAK ROAST ❦ ❦ ❦

| | |
|---|---|
| 1 lb. | top round steak at least 1-inch thick |
| 4 | pork sausages |
| ¼ lb. | ground beef |
| 1 tbsp. | finely chopped onion |
| 1 tbsp. | finely chopped parsley |
| ¼ tsp. | salt |
| Dash | pepper |
| Pinch | dried leaf marjoram |
| Dash | ground nutmeg |
| 2 tbsp. | fine dry bread crumbs |
| 1 | egg |
| 1 tbsp. | tomato paste |
| 4 slices | bacon, cooked until done but not crisp |
| ½ cup | dry red wine |

Trim fat from steak and discard. Split steak along one long side almost through to the other side and open it out flat so you have a thin steak twice the size of the original. Pound with the edge of a heavy plate or with a mallet until about ¼-inch thick.

Heat oven to 450°F. Squeeze meat out of sausage casings and mix with the ground beef, onion, parsley, salt, pepper, marjoram, nutmeg, and bread crumbs.

Beat egg and tomato paste together with a fork and mix into meat mixture. Spread on steak. Cut two of the bacon slices into short strips across the slices and lay them on the ground meat. Roll steak up, wrap remaining two slices of bacon around the roll and tie securely with string in several places. Put in an ungreased baking pan and roast 15 minutes at 450 °F.

Reduce oven temperature to 325 °F, pour wine over meat, cover (you can use foil) and roast until meat is cooked through and very tender, about 1½ hours. Baste often during roasting. Cut in thick slices to serve.

Serves 2 with some left over to serve cold the next day.

**Note:** Splitting the steak is not the easiest thing to do. Try to get your butcher to "butterfly" the steak for you. If you prefer to do it yourself, put the steak in the freezer for about ½ hour before trying to cut it. This will make it firm enough so the job is easier.

## STEAK PIE ❦ ❦ ❦

| | |
|---|---|
| 1 lb. | round steak, cut 1-inch thick |
| 2 tbsp. | flour |
| ½ tsp. | salt |
| ⅛ tsp. | black pepper |
| 2 tbsp. | butter or cooking oil |
| 2 tbsp. | chopped green onions |
| 1 | beef bouillon cube |
| ¾ cup | boiling water |
| ¼ tsp. | salt |
| Dash | pepper |
| 1 | small bay leaf, crumbled |
| 1 tbsp. | chopped parsley |
| ⅛ tsp. | dried leaf marjoram |
| Dash | ground cloves |
| 1½ cups | sliced carrots |
| | Tea Biscuit dough (from Basic Biscuit Mix; see page 175) |
| 1 | egg yolk |
| 1 tbsp. | water |
| 1 tsp. | Worcestershire sauce |

Cut steak into 1-inch cubes. Combine flour, ½ tsp. salt, and ⅛ tsp. pepper in a flat dish. Roll cubes of meat in mixture to coat. Heat butter or oil in a heavy saucepan, add onions, and cook gently 2 minutes, stirring. Add beef cubes and cook, stirring constantly, until browned. Sprinkle in any of the flour mixture left from coating the meat and stir well.

Dissolve bouillon cube in boiling water and add to the meat, along with ¼ tsp. salt, dash pepper, bay leaf, parsley, marjoram, and cloves. Cover and simmer until meat is nearly tender, about 2 hours.

Add carrots and continue simmering, covered, until meat and carrots are tender, about 30 minutes. Turn into 1½ qt. casserole and cool to lukewarm.

Heat oven to 400 °F. Roll biscuit dough into a round slightly larger than the top of the casserole. Lay it on top of the meat and seal well to the sides of the dish. Cut a slit in the dough to let the steam escape.

Beat egg yolk and 1 tbsp. water together with a fork and brush some of mixture on the dough. Bake until biscuit topping is golden brown and meat mixture is bubbling well, about 30 minutes. Remove from oven and spoon the Worcestershire sauce into the pie through the slit in the dough. Serve very hot.

Serves 4.

# ITALIAN STEW, HUNTER'S STYLE 🦃 🦃

| | |
|---|---|
| 1 tbsp. | olive oil |
| ¾ lb. | stewing beef, cubed |
| 2 | small onions, peeled and cut in half |
| 1 | small clove garlic, crushed |
| 2 tbsp. | tomato paste |
| 1 tsp. | flour |
| ¼ tsp. | chili powder |
| ¼ tsp. | dried leaf oregano |
| ¼ tsp. | dried leaf rosemary |
| ¼ tsp. | salt |
| ⅛ tsp. | pepper |
| 2 cups | canned tomatoes |
| 2 tbsp. | chopped parsley |
| ⅓ cup | water |
| 2 | medium carrots, cut into 1-inch pieces |
| ½ cup | elbow macaroni |
| 2 tbsp. | grated Parmesan cheese |

Heat oil in heavy saucepan. Add beef and cook over medium heat, stirring, until lightly browned on all sides. Add onions and garlic and continue stirring 5 minutes. Combine tomato paste, flour, chili powder, oregano, rosemary, salt, and pepper. Stir into mixture in pan along with tomatoes, parsley, and water. Bring to a boil, reduce heat to low, cover, and simmer 1 hour and 15 minutes. Add carrots and continue simmering 45 minutes or until meat is tender.

Cook macaroni according to directions on page 29 while stew is cooking. Rinse under cold running water, then stir into stew at end of cooking time and heat well. Stir in cheese and serve immediately. Good with crusty bread.

Serves 2.

## YANKEE POT ROAST 🦌 🦌

| | |
|---|---|
| 2 tbsp. | cooking oil |
| 3 lb. | pot roast (blade or cross rib) |
| 2 | medium onions, sliced |
| ½ tsp. | salt |
| ¼ tsp. | pepper |
| 1 | bay leaf, crumbled |
| ⅛ tsp. | ground ginger |
| 1 cup | water |
| 1 beef | bouillon cube |
| 1 cup | canned tomatoes |

Heat oil in a heavy saucepan or Dutch oven. Add meat and brown well on all sides. Add onions to one side of pan and stir until they are soft. Add salt, pepper, bay leaf, and ginger; then add water, bouillon cube, and tomatoes. Cover and simmer until meat is very tender, about 2 hours.

Lift meat out of pan and keep hot while you make **Kettle Gravy** (page 80.)

## LAMB CHOPS WITH POTATOES 🦌 🦌

| | |
|---|---|
| 2 | shoulder lamb chops |
| 1 tbsp. | butter or margarine |
| 1 | medium onion, finely chopped |
| 1 | small clove garlic, finely chopped |
| ¼ tsp. | salt |
| Dash | pepper |
| 1 | small bay leaf |
| ½ cup | chicken stock or ½ chicken bouillon cube dissolved in ½ cup boiling water |
| 2 | medium potatoes |
| ¼ tsp. | salt |
| Dash | pepper |
| 1 tbsp. | chopped parsley |
| 2 tsp. | fine, dry bread crumbs |
| 1 tbsp. | butter or margarine |

Trim excess fat from chops. Heat 1 tbsp. butter or margarine in a heavy skillet. Add chops and brown on both sides. Put in a single layer in a small baking dish.

Heat oven to 350°F. Cook onion and garlic in the same skillet, adding a little more butter or margarine if needed. Spoon mixture on top of chops. Sprinkle with ¼ tsp. salt and dash pepper. Break up bay leaf and sprinkle over top of chops. Add chicken stock and cover tightly with foil. Bake 30 minutes.

Peel and slice potatoes very thin. Remove baking dish from oven and spread potatoes over chops. Sprinkle with ¼ tsp. salt and dash pepper. Cover again and bake 30 minutes. Remove from oven.

Combine parsley and bread crumbs and sprinkle over potatoes. Dot with 1 tbsp. butter or margarine, cover, and bake 15 minutes or until chops are very tender. Remove cover and put under hot broiler for a minute or two to lightly brown top of potatoes.

Serves 2.

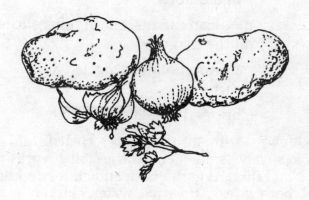

## SKILLET LAMB CHOPS 🐛

| | |
|---|---|
| 2 | shoulder lamb chops |
| | Salt and pepper |
| 2 tbsp. | cooking oil |
| 1 | small clove garlic, cut in half |
| ¼ cup | dry white wine |
| ½ cup | boiling water |
| ½ | chicken bouillon cube |
| 1 strip | lemon rind, cut the length of the lemon with a vegetable peeler |
| 4 | small onions |
| 4 | medium carrots, cut in thick slices on the diagonal |
| 2 | medium potatoes, peeled and quartered |
| | Chopped parsley |

Sprinkle chops with salt and pepper. Heat oil and garlic pieces in a heavy skillet (an electric skillet works well). Lift out and discard garlic, then add chops and brown well on both sides. Add wine, water, chicken bouillon cube, and lemon rind. Cover tightly and simmer until chops begin to get tender, about 30 minutes. Add onions, carrots, and potatoes, sprinkle with salt and pepper, cover again, and simmer about 30 minutes more or until vegetables and meat are all tender. Sprinkle with parsley.

Serves 2.

# VEAL CUTLETS TARRAGON 🐝

| ¾ lb. | thin veal cutlets |
|-------|-------------------|
|       | Flour |
| 1 tbsp. | butter or margarine |
| 1 tbsp. | cooking oil |
| ¼ tsp. | salt |
| ⅛ tsp. | pepper |
| ½ cup | dry white wine |
| ¼ tsp. | dried leaf tarragon |
| 2 tbsp. | dry white wine |

Dip cutlets in flour to lightly coat both sides. Heat butter or margarine and oil in a heavy skillet. Add cutlets and brown quickly. Sprinkle with salt and pepper. Add ½ cup wine and tarragon, reduce heat, and cook, turning the cutlets several times until meat is very tender, about 10 minutes. Put meat on hot platter. Add 2 tbsp. wine to pan and cook quickly 1 minute, scraping up any browned bits. Pour over cutlets.

Serves 2.

## BAKED PORK CHOPS AND APPLES ❦

| | |
|---|---|
| 2 | thick loin pork chops |
| | Salt and pepper |
| 1 | large apple |
| 2 tsp. | grated onion |
| 1 tsp. | sugar |
| ¼ tsp. | ground cinnamon |
| 1 tsp. | butter or margarine |
| Small piece | bay leaf |
| 1 | whole clove |
| ½ cup | apple juice |

Heat oven to 400°F. Have ready a small baking dish just large enough to hold the chops in a single layer.

Trim excess fat from chops and put them in the baking dish. Sprinkle with salt and pepper. Peel and core apple, cut in thin slices, and lay them on top of chops. Sprinkle with onion, then combine sugar and cinnamon and sprinkle over all. Dot with butter or margarine. Add bay leaf and clove to baking dish and pour apple juice over top. Cover tightly with foil and bake about 1½ hours or until chops are tender.

Serves 2.

**To Microwave:** Put chops in baking dish that is suitable for the microwave oven with thickest meaty areas to the edge of dish. Proceed with recipe as directed down to and including pouring apple juice over top. Cover tightly with plastic wrap, turning back one corner to vent, and microwave at medium 35 minutes, or until chops are tender, rotating dish ½ turn after 20 minutes. Let stand, covered, 5 minutes.

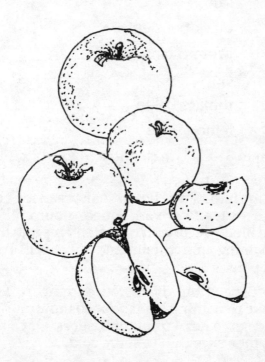

## LAMB LOAF ❧

| | |
|---|---|
| 1½ lb. | ground lean lamb |
| 1 slice | day-old bread |
| 1 | large onion, finely chopped |
| ¼ cup | finely chopped green onions |
| ¼ cup | chopped parsley |
| ¼ cup | chopped celery leaves |
| ½ tsp. | salt |
| ½ tsp. | black pepper |
| ¼ tsp. | ground cinnamon |
| 2 | eggs |
| ¼ cup | tomato paste |
| 1 tbsp. | lemon juice |

Heat oven to 350°F. Grease three 5¾ x 3¼ x 2-inch foil loaf pans.

Put lamb into a large bowl. Soak bread for 2 minutes in enough water to cover. Squeeze out and discard water and break the bread in small pieces into the meat. Add remaining ingredients and mix well. Pack into prepared pans.

Wrap 2 pans tightly in foil and freeze for other meals. Bake remaining loaf about 50 minutes. Drain off liquid and serve hot, cut in thick slices. Or cool, cover, and chill, then slice thin to serve cold.

Each loaf serves 2 if served hot — more if sliced thin and served cold.

# GROUND BEEF AND NOODLES 🦌🦌

| | |
|---|---|
| 2 tbsp. | cooking oil |
| 1 lb. | ground beef |
| 1 cup | chopped onion (1 large) |
| 3 cups | medium noodles (about 4 oz.), uncooked |
| 3 cups | tomato juice |
| 1 tsp. | celery salt |
| Dash | pepper |
| 2 tsp. | Worcestershire sauce |
| 1 cup | thinly sliced celery |
| ½ cup | chopped green pepper |
| 1 cup | plain yogurt or commercial sour cream |
| ½ cup | canned sliced mushrooms, drained |

Heat oil in electric skillet or a regular heavy skillet. Add ground beef and onion and cook gently until beef is lightly browned, stirring constantly and breaking the meat apart. Spread meat and onion evenly in pan and put noodles in a layer on top. Combine tomato juice, celery salt, pepper and Worcestershire sauce and pour over noodles. Bring to a boil, reduce heat, cover and simmer 20 minutes. Add celery and green pepper, cover again, and simmer 10 minutes or until noodles are tender and vegetables are tender-crisp. Stir in yogurt or sour cream and mushrooms and heat but do not boil. Serve immediately.

Makes 4 servings.

# HAM AND MACARONI CASSEROLE 🐸 🐸

| | |
|---|---|
| ⅔ cup | uncooked elbow macaroni |
| 1 | egg white |
| 1 | egg yolk |
| 1 tbsp. | butter or margarine, melted |
| ¾ cup | coarsely chopped cooked ham (see note) |
| 1 tbsp. | melted butter or margarine |
| ½ cup | ¼-inch day-old bread cubes |
| ¼ cup | coarsely grated process cheese |
| 1 tsp. | butter or margarine |
| 1 | green onion with top, thinly sliced |
| ½ cup | sliced mushrooms |
| 2 tbsp. | tomato paste |
| ½ cup | water |
| 2 tsp. | lemon juice |

Heat oven to 375°F. Butter a 1-qt. casserole generously.

Cook macaroni according to directions on page 29. Drain. Beat egg white until stiff. Beat egg yolk. Stir 1 tbsp. melted butter or margarine and ham into egg yolk, then combine with macaroni. Fold in egg white and put into prepared casserole.

Combine 1 tbsp. melted butter or margarine and bread cubes, tossing with a fork so bread cubes are coated with butter. Add cheese and toss with a fork. Sprinkle over top of the macaroni mixture.

Bake about 30 minutes or until mixture is set in the middle and nicely browned on top. (If using a toaster oven it may be necessary to cover with foil so it doesn't brown too much on top.)

Heat 1 tsp. butter or margarine in a small saucepan while the casserole bakes. Add onion and mushrooms and cook and stir over medium heat 3 minutes. Add tomato paste, water, and lemon juice. Heat well and pour over servings.

Serves 2.

**Note:** This recipe is good for using leftover ham. You can substitute canned flakes of ham if you wish.

## SEPARATING AN EGG

Separating an egg yolk from the white is easy. Break the shell with a sharp tap with the blade of a knife or on the edge of a bowl and pull the shell halves apart with the tips of your thumbs, keeping the yolk in one half and letting the white run out into a bowl. Then turn the yolk back and forth between the halves of shell to let the rest of the white run out. If you get a small amount of the yolk in the white, just dip it out with the egg shell.

# CREAMY MACARONI AND CHEESE 🐦 🐦

| | |
|---|---|
| 1 cup | elbow macaroni |
| 2 slices | bacon, cut in small pieces |
| 1 tbsp. | butter or margarine |
| 2 tbsp. | flour |
| ⅛ tsp. | pepper |
| ¼ tsp. | dry mustard |
| Pinch | ground nutmeg |
| ⅓ cup | skim milk powder |
| 1 cup | water |
| 1 cup | frozen peas |
| ¾ cup | grated process cheese |
| 1 tbsp. | butter or margarine, melted (optional) |
| ¼ cup | fine, dry bread crumbs (optional) |

Cook macaroni according to directions on page 29. Drain.

Cook bacon in medium saucepan until crisp, stirring constantly. Drain off excess fat and add 1 tbsp. butter or margarine to pan. Sprinkle in flour, stir to blend, and remove from heat. Stir in pepper, mustard, nutmeg, and skim milk powder. Stir in water gradually. Add frozen peas and set over medium heat and cook until boiling, thickened, and smooth, stirring gently. Turn heat to low and simmer 5 minutes, stirring often. Add cheese and stir until melted, then stir in macaroni. Heat through.

Serve at this point if desired. Or, if you prefer, heat oven to 400°F, pour macaroni mixture into a buttered 1-qt. casserole, top with a mixture of the melted butter or margarine and crumbs, and bake 10 minutes or until topping is lightly browned.

Serves 2 to 4.

**To Microwave:** Cook macaroni according to directions below. Drain. Cut bacon into 1-qt. casserole and cover loosely with waxed paper. Microwave at high about 2 minutes. Drain off excess fat. Add 1 tbsp. butter or margarine to casserole and microwave 10 seconds to melt. Stir in next 5 ingredients, then stir in water gradually. Microwave at high about 3 minutes, stirring with a fork once every minute, until thick. Add cheese and stir with fork until cheese is melted, then stir in peas and macaroni. Mix well, cover, and microwave at medium high about 4 minutes, stirring after 2 minutes, until very hot. Let stand 3 minutes, then serve.

## TO MICROWAVE PASTA

For 2 people, put 4 oz. (1 cup) uncooked pasta in a 1½-qt. casserole. Add 3 cups boiling water and 1 tsp. salt, stir, then microwave on high (10), uncovered, about 6 minutes. Stir once during cooking. Remove from oven, cover tightly, and let stand 10 minutes. Drain and serve.

# PLAIN MACARONI AND CHEESE 🦃 🦃

| | |
|---|---|
| 1 cup | elbow macaroni |
| 1½ tbsp. | butter or margarine |
| ½ tsp. | finely grated onion |
| 1½ tbsp. | flour |
| ½ tsp. | garlic salt |
| Dash | black pepper |
| Dash | cayenne |
| ⅛ tsp. | dry mustard |
| 1 cup | milk |
| ¾ cup | grated old cheddar cheese |
| 2 tbsp. | grated Parmesan cheese |
| 2 tbsp. | chopped parsley |
| 1 tbsp. | chopped pimento (optional) |

Cook macaroni according to directions on page 29. Drain.

Heat butter or margarine in a medium saucepan over medium heat, add onion and stir 3 minutes. Sprinkle in flour, garlic salt, pepper, cayenne, and mustard. Stir to blend, remove from heat, and add milk all at once. Stir and return to heat. Cook, stirring constantly, until thick and smooth. Add cheeses and heat gently just until melted. Stir in macaroni and heat well. Add parsley and pimento and serve immediately.

Serves 2.

# CORNED BEEF PATTIES 🐛 🐛

| | |
|---|---|
| ½ can (12-oz. size) | corned beef |
| 2 tsp. | butter or margarine |
| 1 | small onion, finely chopped |
| 1 tbsp. | finely chopped green pepper |
| 1 cup | diced cooked potatoes |
| ½ cup | canned whole kernel corn, drained |
| 1 | egg, beaten |
| 2 tbsp. | flour |
| ¼ tsp. | baking powder |
| 1 tbsp. | butter or margarine |

Break up corned beef finely into a bowl. Melt 2 tsp. butter or margarine in a small skillet. Add onion and green pepper and cook over medium heat, stirring, 3 minutes. Add to corned beef along with all remaining ingredients except 1 tbsp. butter or margarine. Blend very well with a fork. Shape into 4 patties with hands. (The mixture will be quite soft. If you have trouble handling it, flour your hands well). Heat remaining 1 tbsp. butter or margarine in heavy skillet and fry patties slowly until golden on both sides. Makes 4 medium patties.

Serves 2 or 4.

**Note:** I have difficulty finding the small size corned beef cans, but if you can find them, they are just right for this recipe.

# CHICKEN IN SPICY ORANGE SAUCE ❦ ❦ ❦

| | |
|---|---|
| 2 | whole chicken breasts, cut in half to make 4 sides |
| 1 tbsp. | cooking oil |
| ¼ cup | flour |
| ¼ tsp. | salt |
| ⅛ tsp. | pepper |
| ¼ tsp. | paprika |
| 1 | medium onion, chopped |
| 1 | large clove garlic, minced |
| 1 cup | chicken stock |
| ¾ cup | orange juice |
| 1 | small green pepper, seeded and cut in strips |
| | Grated rind of 1 orange |
| ¼ tsp. | crushed red peppers |
| ½ tsp. | ground cumin (optional) |
| ½ tsp. | dried leaf oregano |
| 1 tbsp. | lemon juice |
| 2 tbsp. | chopped parsley |
| 4 thin slices | orange |
| | Chopped parsley |

Skin and bone chicken pieces. (You can buy them already prepared but it's nice to have the bones to make stock.)

Heat oil in a heavy skillet. Combine flour, salt, pepper, and paprika in a flat dish and roll chicken pieces in mixture. Reserve any excess flour.

Brown the chicken in the oil, adding more oil as needed. Put the chicken in a baking dish measuring about 12 x 7 x 2 inches Add onion and garlic to fat left in pan and stir until soft. Sprinkle in any flour left from coating chicken and stir to blend. Remove from heat and stir in chicken stock and orange juice. Return to medium heat and add green pepper, orange rind, red peppers, cumin, oregano, lemon juice, and 2 tbsp. parsley. Stir until boiling, slightly thickened, and smooth. Pour over chicken. Cover baking dish with foil.

Heat oven to 375 °F. Bake about 40 minutes or until chicken is very tender. Garnish with orange slices and more chopped parsley.

Serves 4.

**To Microwave:** Prepare chicken as directed down to and including pouring orange sauce over chicken pieces. Cover with transparent wrap, turning back one corner to vent, and microwave at high for 11 to 13 minutes.

## STUFFED CHICKEN BREAST 🐦 🐦

| | |
|---|---|
| 1 | large whole chicken breast (cut in half to make two sides) |
| 2 tbsp. | butter or margarine |
| 1 tbsp. | finely chopped onion |
| 1 tbsp. | finely chopped celery leaves |
| 2 cups | day-old bread cubes |
| Pinch | salt |
| Dash | pepper |
| 2 tsp. | chopped parsley |
| ½ tsp. | poultry seasoning |
| Pinch | dried leaf marjoram |
| | Paprika |
| 2 tbsp. | melted butter or margarine |

Heat oven to 350°F. Butter a small, shallow baking dish just large enough to hold 1 of the chicken pieces.

Skin and bone chicken pieces and put between 2 sheets of waxed paper, skinned side up, and pound with a rolling pin or mallet until each piece of meat is about twice the size you started with. Put 1 piece of chicken in the baking dish, skinned side down.

Heat 2 tbsp. butter or margarine in a small skillet over medium heat. Add onion and celery leaves and stir for 3 minutes. Add half the bread cubes and continue stirring until cubes are lightly browned. Add to remaining bread cubes along with salt, pepper, parsley, poultry seasoning, and marjoram. Toss together, then spread on chicken piece in baking dish. Lay the other

piece of chicken on top, skinned si
chicken together to seal. Sprinkle
paprika and drizzle with 2 tbsp. melted
garine.

Bake 30 minutes, turn, and sprinkle with
Add a little more melted butter or margarine if
dry. Continue baking until very tender, about
minutes, basting often with drippings in pan or with
extra butter or margarine. Cut in half to serve.

Serves 2.

roni (or use bows or

rine

le up. Press edges of
generously with
butter or mar-

paprika.
pan is
30

onion

| ¼ tsp. | salt |
| ¼ tsp. | black pepper |
| ¼ tsp. | dried leaf thyme |
| 1 cup | chicken stock |
| 1 cup | cut up cooked chicken |
| ¼ | cup light cream |
| 2 tbsp. | chopped parsley |
| 2 tbsp. | lemon juice |
| ¼ cup | chopped, toasted almonds |
| ¼ cup | fine, dry bread crumbs |
| 2 tbsp. | melted butter or margarine |

Cook macaroni according to package directions or follow directions on page 29.

Heat oven to 350 °F. Butter a 1-qt. casserole.

Heat 2 tbsp. butter or margarine in a medium saucepan, add curry powder, and cook gently, stirring, 1 minute. Add celery and onion and cook gently 3 minutes more. Sprinkle in flour, salt, pepper, and thyme and stir to blend. Remove from heat, add stock, and stir to blend. Return to heat and cook until boiling, thickened, and smooth. Stir in macaroni and all remaining ingredients except almonds, crumbs, and 2 tbsp. melted butter or margarine. Turn into prepared casserole. Combine almonds, crumbs, and melted butter or margarine and sprinkle over all. Bake 20 minutes or until very hot and bubbling.

Serves 2 to 4.

**To Microwave:** Cook macaroni as directed on page 101. Put butter or margarine in 1-qt. casserole and microwave at high until melted. Stir in curry powder and microwave at high for 10 seconds. Add celery and onion, stir, cover, and microwave at high 2 minutes. Stir in flour, salt, pepper, and thyme, then add chicken stock gradually. Microwave at high 4 minutes, stirring with a fork once every minute. Stir in macaroni, chicken, cream, parsley, and lemon juice. Sprinkle with a mixture of almonds, bread crumbs and melted butter or margarine. Cover and microwave at high 4 minutes or until hot. Let stand 4 minutes, covered, then serve.

# POACHED SALMON WITH CUCUMBER SAUCE 🦃 🦃

| | |
|---|---|
| ⅓ cup | plain yogurt |
| ¼ cup | finely chopped peeled and seeded cucumber |
| 2 tbsp. | chopped parsley |
| 1 cup | water (or ½ cup water and ½ cup dry white wine) |
| 1 | chicken bouillon cube |
| 1 tbsp. | white vinegar |
| 1 | small onion, sliced |
| Small piece | bay leaf |
| Sprig | parsley |
| Sprig | fresh dill (or ½ tsp. dried dill weed) |
| 2 | peppercorns |
| 2 | small salmon steaks, about ¾-inch thick |

Combine yogurt, cucumber, and chopped parsley and refrigerate.

Heat water to boiling in a small skillet (use more liquid — up to 2 cups — if skillet is large). Add bouillon cube and stir until dissolved. Add remaining ingredients except salmon and bring to a boil. Turn heat to medium-low, cover, and simmer 5 minutes.

Add salmon, cover and simmer 6 to 8 minutes or until fish is cooked through (check at backbone). Lift steaks out onto a hot platter with an egg turner. Lift onions out and lay over fish. Serve immediately with chilled yogurt-cucumber mixture.

Serves 2.

**Note:** Strain the cooking liquid from the fish and freeze it to use in fish soup another day.

**To Microwave:** Heat water or water and wine in a baking dish just large enough to hold the salmon steaks in a single layer at high 1 minute. Add bouillon cube and stir to dissolve. Stir in all remaining ingredients except salmon. Put salmon steaks in baking dish, thick sides to edge. Cover tightly and microwave at high 2 minutes. Turn baking dish ½ turn and microwave 2 to 3 minutes more or until small ends of steaks flake easily. Let stand covered 3 minutes, then serve with yogurt-cucumber mixture.

# SALMON AND RICE CASSEROLE 🐟 🐟

| | |
|---|---|
| 7½-oz. can | pink salmon |
| 3 slices | bacon, cut up |
| ¼ cup | finely chopped onion |
| ½ cup | regular long grain rice |
| 1½ cups | boiling water |
| 1 cup | thinly sliced celery |
| ½ cup | slivered green pepper |
| 1 cup | frozen peas |
| ¼ cup | chopped parsley |
| 2 tbsp. | butter or margarine |
| 2 tbsp. | flour |
| ¼ tsp. | salt |
| ⅛ tsp. | pepper |
| 1½ cups | liquid (salmon liquid plus milk) |

Drain salmon, saving liquid. Fry bacon bits in medium saucepan. Lift out with a slotted spoon, then add onion and rice to bacon drippings in saucepan and cook gently, stirring, until rice is golden. Add boiling water, cover, and simmer 15 minutes. Add celery and green pepper, mix lightly with a fork, cover again, and simmer about 10 minutes or until vegetables are tender-crisp and water is absorbed. Remove from heat and stir in peas, bacon bits, and parsley. Flake salmon and stir in lightly with fork.

Heat oven to 375°F. Butter a shallow baking dish (about 10 x 6 x 1¾ inches). Melt butter or margarine in saucepan. Sprinkle in flour, salt, and pepper and stir to blend. Remove from heat and stir in liquid all at once. Return to medium heat and cook and stir until boiling, thickened, and smooth. Pour a thin layer of sauce into baking dish, using about a third of the sauce. Add half of salmon-rice mixture. Repeat layers and top with a final layer of sauce. Bake 30 minutes or until bubbling well.

Makes 4 servings.

## TO MICROWAVE FISH

Since fish is naturally tender, it needs minimum cooking. (If fish is frozen, thaw completely before cooking.) If the outside is opaque and the center not quite done, it's fine. The center will finish cooking while the fish stands for a short time. For 1 or 2 fillets or steaks about ½-inch thick, you should need only 3 or 4 minutes at high power. Put steaks on paper towel in baking dish, brush with melted butter or margarine, sprinkle with lemon juice and dill if desired, and cover loosely with waxed paper. Microwave minimum time, then check to see if fish flakes easily.

Or, for whole, small fish, such as trout, brush fish with melted butter or margarine in baking dish. If you are leaving the head and tail on, it is all right to wrap them with foil. Cover the baking dish tightly with transparent wrap and turn back one corner to vent. Microwave on high (10). A small trout weighing about ½ lb. takes only 3 to 4 minutes.

# OVEN FRIED FISH 🐟 🐟

| ¾ to 1 lb. | fresh or frozen fish fillets (sole, haddock, or cod) |
| --- | --- |
| ¼ cup | buttermilk |
| ¼ tsp. | salt |
| ⅛ tsp. | pepper |
| ¼ tsp. | dried leaf thyme |
| ¼ cup | fine, dry bread crumbs |
| 1 tbsp. | finely chopped parsley |
| 1 tbsp. | cooking oil |
| | Tartar Sauce (page 78) |

If using frozen fish, thaw until fillets can be separated easily.

Heat oven to 500°F. Oil a small glass baking dish.

Combine buttermilk, salt, pepper, and thyme in a flat dish and crumbs and parsley in another. Dip fish into buttermilk mixture, then in crumbs to coat both sides. Lay in prepared baking dish in a single layer. Drizzle with oil.

Bake 5 minutes for fresh fish, 10 minutes for frozen or until fish flakes easily with a fork. Do not turn. Serve immediately with **Tartar Sauce.**

Serves 2.

## GOLDEN SOLE ❦

| | |
|---|---|
| ¾ lb. | fillet of sole |
| | Pepper |
| 2 tbsp. | butter or margarine, melted |
| ¼ cup | grated Parmesan cheese |
| ⅛ tsp. | dried leaf thyme |

Heat oven to 400°F. Cut the fish into 2 serving-size pieces. Put a piece of heavy foil just a little larger than the two pieces of fish on a cookie sheet and turn the edges of the foil up to form a dish.

Sprinkle fish lightly with pepper, then brush one side with half the butter or margarine. Combine cheese and thyme and sprinkle half of this mixture on the buttered side of the fish, patting it down lightly. Turn fish onto foil, cheese side down. Brush second side with butter or margarine and sprinkle with cheese mixture.

Bake about 10 minutes or until very lightly browned. Baste with any butter or margarine that collects in the foil but do not turn. Serve immediately.

Serves 2.

# FISH ROLLS 🦃🦃

| | |
|---|---|
| ¾ lb. | cod fillets |
| 1½ tbsp. | drained sweet pickle relish |
| 1 tbsp. | finely chopped onion |
| 1 tbsp. | butter or margarine |
| 1 tbsp. | flour |
| ¼ tsp. | salt |
| Dash | pepper |
| ¾ cup | milk |
| ½ tsp. | Worcestershire sauce |
| ¼ cup | grated old cheddar cheese |
| 1 tbsp. | grated old cheddar cheese |

Heat oven to 350°F. Butter a 20-oz. casserole or small baking dish.

Split fillets lengthwise along natural dividing lines (if fillets are very thick, split horizontally too), then cut into pieces about 6 inches long. You should have about 4 pieces, 6 x 1½ inches.

Combine relish and onion and spread some of the mixture on each piece of fish and roll up like a cinnamon roll, fastening with a toothpick. Put in baking dish.

Melt butter or margarine in a small saucepan over medium heat. Sprinkle in flour, salt, and pepper and stir to blend.

Remove from heat and stir in milk and Worcestershire sauce. Return to heat and stir until boiling, thickened, and smooth.

Remove from heat and stir in ¼ cup cheese. Pour over fish and sprinkle with remaining 1 tbsp. cheese.

Bake until fish flakes easily with a fork, about 20 minutes.

Serves 2.

## CREAMED SALMON ON TOAST 🦐 🦐

| | |
|---|---|
| 7½-oz. can | pink salmon |
| 2 tbsp. | butter or margarine |
| 2 tbsp. | flour |
| ¼ tsp. | salt |
| Dash | pepper |
| 1 cup | milk plus salmon liquid |
| | Chopped parsley (optional) |
| 2 | slices whole wheat toast |

Drain salmon, saving liquid. Break salmon into bite-size pieces. (The bones are soft, so mash and add them to the sauce for extra nutrition.)

Heat butter or margarine in a saucepan. Sprinkle in flour, salt, and pepper and stir to blend. Remove from heat and add milk and salmon liquid all at once, stirring to blend. Return to medium-high heat and stir until boiling, thickened, and smooth. Turn heat to low and add salmon pieces. Heat, stirring gently so as not to break up salmon, until salmon is warmed through. Stir in parsley and serve on toast.

Serves 2.

## TWO-EGG OMELET 🦐 🦐

| | |
|---|---|
| 2 | eggs |
| 1 tbsp. | water |
| ⅛ tsp. | salt |
| | Fresh ground black pepper |
| 1 tbsp. | butter or margarine |
| 1 tbsp. | chopped parsley (optional) |

Beat eggs, water, salt, and pepper together with a fork just until blended but not foamy. Set aside.

Heat omelet pan or skillet over high heat until very hot (a drop of water skitters around on the surface). Add butter or margarine and heat until foamy but not brown. (Lift pan off heat if fat starts to brown.) Swish fat around to coat bottom and part way up sides of pan, add parsley, and pour in the egg mixture.

Hold the handle of the pan in one hand (the left if you are right-handed), the fork, flat side down, in the other. As soon as the eggs start to set (instantly if the pan is the right temperature) stir right around the pan, shaking it back and forth to keep the omelet free. Continue cooking and shaking, stirring around the pan only enough to let the uncooked egg run under the cooked, until the egg is almost set but still moist on top, about 30 seconds. Let the egg cook 2 seconds without stirring so it browns lightly, shaking the pan back and forth to keep the omelet free. Tilt the pan over a hot plate so the omelet rolls down toward the side opposite the handle, and push it with the fork so it rolls up neatly out onto the plate.

Serves 1.

## VARIATIONS:

### Ham Omelet

Mix ¼ cup finely chopped cooked ham, 1 tbsp. each finely chopped green onion and green pepper, and sprinkle over cooked omelet just before rolling it out of the pan.

### Cheese Omelet

Just before rolling it out of the pan, sprinkle omelet with ¼ cup grated old cheddar cheese.

**Note:** If you really love omelets and intend to make them often, an investment in a good omelet pan is worth it. It should be 7 or 8 inches in diameter (for a two- or three-egg omelet), fairly heavy in weight, with a long handle and rounded sloping sides so the omelet can slide around and out of the pan easily. I find I can use my skillet with a non-stick coating and sloping sides quite successfully.

Making a good omelet takes coordination; you need to shake the pan with one hand and stir with the other. It's easy once you've done it a couple of times. Read through the recipe carefully so you are sure you know just what to do, then work without stopping for the most tender and delicious omelet.

## FINNAN HADDIE WITH EGG SAUCE ❦ ❦

| | |
|---|---|
| ½ | small onion, sliced paper thin |
| ½ tsp. | peppercorns |
| ¾ to 1 lb. | finnan haddie, cut into 2 servings |
| 1½ cups | milk |
| 2 tbsp. | butter or margarine |
| 1½ tbsp. | flour |
| ½ tsp. | lemon juice |
| 1½ tsp. | butter or margarine |
| 1 | hard-cooked egg, chopped (see page 20) |

Separate onion slices into rings and sprinkle them over the bottom of a heavy skillet or saucepan. Add peppercorns and lay fish on top. Add milk (fish should be covered), bring to a boil, turn down heat, cover, and simmer about 10 minutes or until fish flakes easily with a fork. Lift fish out with a slotted spoon and put on hot platter. Strain cooking liquid and measure out 1 cup for the sauce. Discard any remaining liquid.

Heat cooking liquid in saucepan. Cream 2 tbsp. butter or margarine and flour together and add to hot liquid bit by bit, stirring well after each addition. Cook over medium heat, stirring constantly, until boiling, thickened, and smooth. Turn down heat and continue cooking and stirring 3 minutes. Stir in lemon juice, 1½ tsp. butter or margarine, and chopped egg.

Serve fish with egg sauce spooned over top.

Serves 2.

# TO MICROWAVE EGGS

Never try to cook an egg in its shell in the microwave as it will explode. Always puncture the yolks three times with the tip of a sharp knife before cooking unless the eggs have been beaten. Since all foods cooked in the microwave continue cooking after they come out of the oven, to have perfect eggs you should cook them to slightly underdone.

To microwave fried eggs, put ¼ tsp. butter or margarine in a custard cup. Melt in microwave oven. Add an egg to cup, puncture the yolk in three places, sprinkle lightly with salt and generously with pepper, cover with waxed paper and cook on high for 30 seconds. Let stand 1 minute then serve. For 2 eggs you will need to cook about 1 minute and let stand 1 minute. To microwave a poached egg, heat ½ cup water and ½ tsp. white vinegar to boiling in the microwave oven in a 10-oz. custard cup. Break egg into a small dish and puncture the yolk three times. Slip the egg into the boiling water, cover with waxed paper, and cook on high for 25 seconds. Let stand, covered, 1 minute, then lift out onto toast to serve. Two eggs will need 1 cup water, 1 tsp. vinegar in a 20-oz. custard cup, 1 minute cooking time, and 1 minute standing time.

To microwave a scrambled egg, beat egg, 1 tsp. soft butter, and 1 tbsp. cream or milk lightly with a fork in a 6-oz. custard cup. Cook 30 seconds on high, stir with a fork, and cook 15 to 30 seconds longer. Let stand 1 minute. For 2 eggs, use a 10-oz. custard cup, 2 tsp. butter, and 2 tbsp. cream or milk. Cooking times will be about 45 seconds and 30 seconds.

## COTTAGE EGGS ❧ ❧ ❧

| | |
|---|---|
| 1½ cups | cooked rice (see page 33) |
| 3 | hard-cooked eggs (see page 20) |
| ¼ cup | cream-style cottage cheese |
| 1 tbsp. | light mayonnaise |
| 1 tbsp. | each finely chopped radish, celery, cucumber, and green pepper |
| Pinch | salt |
| Dash | pepper |
| 2 tbsp. | butter or margarine |
| 1 tbsp. | finely chopped onion |
| 2 tbsp. | flour |
| 1 cup | milk |
| ¼ tsp. | salt |
| Dash | pepper |
| 1 tbsp. | chopped parsley |

Heat oven to 350 °F. Butter a baking dish about 8 x 6 x 2 inches.

Spread rice in prepared baking dish. Cut eggs in half lengthwise, lift out yolks, put them in a bowl, and mash them well with a fork. Add cottage cheese and mayonnaise and mash until smooth. Stir in radish, celery, cucumber, green pepper, pinch salt, and dash pepper. Fill egg whites with mixture, piling high and set on top of rice in baking dish.

Melt butter or margarine in medium saucepan over medium heat. Add onion and stir 3 minutes. Sprinkle in flour and stir to blend. Remove from heat and add milk all at once. Stir in ¼ tsp. salt and dash pepper. Return to heat and stir until boiling, thickened, and smooth. Stir in parsley and pour over eggs.

Bake until very hot, about 20 minutes.

Serves 2.

## DUTCH SCRAMBLE ❦

| | |
|---|---|
| 2 slices | day-old bread |
| 3 tbsp. | butter or margarine |
| 1 tsp. | finely grated onion |
| 6 | eggs |
| 6 tbsp. | light cream |
| ¼ tsp. | salt |
| ¼ tsp. | pepper |

Cut crusts from bread and cut bread into ¼-inch cubes. Heat butter or margarine in a heavy skillet, add the bread cubes and onion, and cook gently, stirring, until cubes are golden.

Beat eggs, cream, salt, and pepper together with a fork. Pour into pan and stir once around with the fork. Let cook gently over low heat, lifting and turning mixture around the sides and bottom as it sets. Remove from heat as soon as cooked through but still moist and glossy. Serve immediately.

Serves 3.

# EASY HAM-ZUCCHINI PIE 🐛

| | |
|---|---|
| 1 cup | small, thin slices zucchini |
| ½ cup | ground leftover ham or canned flakes of ham |
| ¼ cup | grated Swiss or cheddar cheese |
| 1 tbsp. | grated onion |
| 1 | egg |
| Dash | each salt, pepper, and nutmeg |
| 3 tbsp. | biscuit mix (commercial or Basic Biscuit Mix; page 174) |
| ⅔ cup | milk |

Heat oven to 350°F. Grease 2 foil tart pans generously (4½ to 5-inches in diameter).

Spread zucchini slices in the prepared pans. Combine ham, cheese, and onion and spread over zucchini layer. Put remaining ingredients in the glass of the blender and blend at high speed 30 seconds. Pour over ham mixture.

Bake 35 minutes or until a knife inserted near the center comes out clean. Let stand 5 minutes and serve. Good cold too.

Serves 2.

**Note:** Substitute flaked tuna for the ham if desired.

# SALADS AND VEGETABLES

# SALADS AND VEGETABLES

What is more delicious than a crisp, colorful salad? And what accents a good meal better than perfectly cooked vegetables?

Both fruits and vegetables supply vitamin A (for normal bone development, maintenance of skin and lining membrane, and good night vision), vitamin C (for healthy teeth and gums and strong blood vessels), thiamin (for healthy nervous system and digestive tract), folic acid (for formation of hemoglobin in red blood cells — asparagus, beets, broccoli, brussels sprouts, and spinach are good sources), iron (an essential part of hemoglobin), and carbohydrates (starch, sugar, and fiber are all essential in moderate amounts to supply energy and provide roughage).

Because vegetables, particularly the leafy green and yellow vegetables, have more vitamin A, folacin (folic acid), and iron than fruits, at least two servings of vegetables are recommended for your daily diet. Personally, I'd recommend more — just because they are so good to eat!

The recipes for salads here include vegetable salads, fruit salads, several slaws, and salads containing meat and fish, as well as a choice of dressings. And the vegetable recipes range from A to Z: asparagus to zucchini.

# CAESAR SALAD 🐞 🐞

| | |
|---|---|
| 1 tbsp. | butter or margarine |
| 2 tsp. | salad oil |
| 1 small clove | garlic, peeled and cut in half |
| 1 slice | day-old bread, cut in ¼-inch cubes |
| 2 slices | bacon |
| | Salt |
| 1 small clove | garlic, peeled and cut in half |
| 4 cups | torn-up romaine lettuce |
| 1 tbsp. | chopped anchovies (optional) |
| 1½ tbsp. | salad oil |
| 2 tsp. | lemon juice |
| Pinch | salt |
| Dash | black pepper |
| 1 | egg |
| 1 tbsp. | grated Parmesan cheese |

Heat butter or margarine and 2 tsp. oil in a small skillet. Add 1 clove garlic and cook gently, stirring, 1 minute. Add bread cubes and cook over medium heat, stirring, until golden. Lift out bread cubes with a slotted spoon and drain on paper towelling. Discard garlic. Add bacon strips to same pan and cook until crisp, then drain on paper towelling and crumble.

Sprinkle salad bowl lightly with salt, then rub cut sides of 1 clove garlic in the salt and all over the bottom and sides of the bowl. Discard garlic. Put the romaine, anchovies, and browned bread cubes in the bowl and toss together lightly.

Combine 1½ tbsp. oil, lemon juice, pinch salt, dash pepper, and egg in a small jar with a tight lid. Shake together until well blended, then pour over greens and toss lightly. Sprinkle bacon bits and cheese over top of salad and serve immediately.

Serves 2.

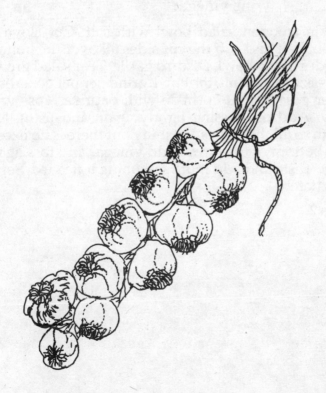

## TOSSED GREEN SALAD ❦

|  | Salt |
| --- | --- |
| 1 clove | garlic |
| 3 cups | torn-up mixed salad greens |
|  | Fresh ground black pepper |
|  | Paprika (optional) |
| 1½ tbsp. (approx-) | olive oil |
| 2 tsp. | wine vinegar |

Sprinkle wooden salad bowl with salt. Cut clove of garlic in half and rub the cut sides all over the bottom and sides of the bowl. Discard garlic. Tear salad greens in bite-size pieces into the bowl, grind pepper generously over greens, and sprinkle with paprika. Toss very lightly. Add oil, tossing lightly again and using just enough so all the leaves are shiny but there is no excess in the bottom of the bowl. Add vinegar and toss again lightly. Taste and add more seasoning if needed. Serve immediately.

Serves 2.

# CARROT-SPROUT SALAD 🐿

| | |
|---|---|
| 2 tbsp. | light mayonnaise |
| 1 tbsp. | chopped parsley |
| 1 tsp. | soya sauce |
| ¼ | tsp. sugar |
| ⅛ | tsp. pepper |
| | Boiling water |
| ½ pkg. (10-oz. size) | frozen frenched green beans |
| 1 cup | fresh bean sprouts |
| ¾ cup | grated carrots (use medium grater) |
| | Lettuce |

Combine mayonnaise, parsley, soya sauce, sugar, and pepper. Chill.

Add a small amount of boiling water to green beans in a saucepan. Bring to a boil over high heat, cover, and boil 1 minute. Drain immediately, then chill.

At serving time, rinse bean sprouts under cold running water and drain well. Combine with carrots and beans. Add mayonnaise mixture and toss lightly. Serve on lettuce.

Serves 2.

## EASY SUMMER SALAD ❦

| | |
|---|---|
| ¼ cup | mayonnaise-type salad dressing |
| 1 tsp. | sugar |
| Dash | salt |
| ¾ tsp. | grated lemon rind |
| 1½ tsp. | lemon juice |
| 3 to 4 cups | torn-up leaf lettuce |
| ½ cup | paper-thin slices radishes |
| ½ cup | ¼-inch cubes old cheddar cheese |

Combine mayonnaise, sugar, salt, lemon rind, and juice. Chill well. At serving time, combine remaining ingredients, add the dressing, and toss lightly.

Serves 2 generously.

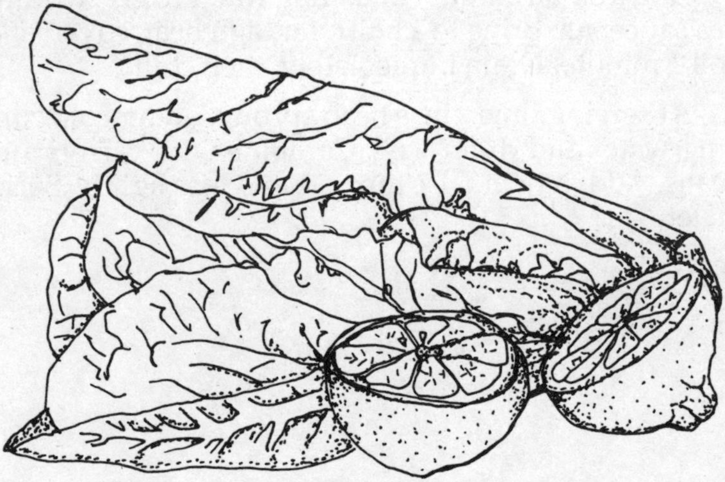

# MUSHROOM SALAD 🍎

| | |
|---|---|
| ¼ cup | olive or salad oil |
| ¼ cup | cider vinegar |
| 1 tbsp. | finely chopped green onion |
| 1 tbsp. | chopped parsley |
| 1 small clove | garlic, slightly crushed |
| ¼ tsp. | salt |
| ¼ tsp. | sugar |
| 1½ cups | sliced fresh mushrooms |
| | Leaf or Boston lettuce |
| | Parsley sprigs |

Combine oil, vinegar, onion, 1 tbsp. parsley, garlic, salt, and sugar in a medium jar with a tight lid. Shake to blend well. Add sliced mushrooms and turn upside down two or three times to mix dressing well with mushrooms. Refrigerate at least 1½ hours, turning upside down once or twice.

Drain mushrooms at serving time, saving marinade for dressing greens for another meal. Discard garlic. Spoon mushrooms onto lettuce to serve and garnish with parsley.

Serves 2.

## ORANGE AND ONION SALAD ❦

| | |
|---|---|
| 1 | medium red onion, sliced paper thin |
| 1 | large orange, peeled and sliced thin |
| | Lettuce |
| | Tarragon French Dressing (page 141) |

Soak onion slices in salted ice water for 15 minutes. Drain. Arrange onion and orange slices alternately on lettuce. Pass the **Tarragon French Dressing.**

Serves 2.

## AVOCADO-ORANGE SALAD ❦

| | |
|---|---|
| 1 tbsp. | salad oil |
| 1 tsp. | lime or lemon juice |
| 1 tsp. | white vinegar |
| Dash | salt |
| Dash | white pepper |
| 1 | avocado |
| 1 | large orange |
| | Lettuce leaves |

Combine oil, lime or lemon juice, vinegar, salt, and pepper in a small jar with a tight lid and shake to blend well. Peel and slice avocado and orange thinly. Cover 2 salad plates with lettuce and top with overlapping slices of avocado and orange. Drizzle with oil mixture. Serve immediately.

Serves 2.

## ZUCCHINI AND TOMATO SALAD 🦌

| | |
|---|---|
| ¼ cup | light mayonnaise |
| 1 tsp. | prepared mustard |
| 2 tsp. | chopped chives |
| ¼ tsp. | salt |
| Dash | pepper |
| 1 | large tomato, peeled, seeded, and diced coarsely (about 1 cup) |
| 1 cup | unpeeled, diced raw zucchini |
| 2 | green onions, sliced thin |
| | Lettuce |

Combine mayonnaise, mustard, chives, salt, and pepper, blending well.

Put tomato, zucchini, and onions in a bowl, add mayonnaise mixture, and toss to blend well. Chill a few minutes.

Cover 2 plates with lettuce and spoon on salad at serving time.

Serves 2.

# MACARONI AND CHEESE SALAD 🦞

| | |
|---|---|
| ½ cup | elbow macaroni |
| ¼ tsp. | salt |
| ¼ cup | grated old cheddar cheese |
| 1 tbsp. | commercial French dressing |
| ½ cup | thinly sliced celery |
| 2 tbsp. | thinly sliced green onions |
| 2 tbsp. | mayonnaise |
| 1 tbsp. | sweet pickle relish |
| 3¾-oz. can | tuna, flaked |
| | Lettuce |

Cook macaroni with salt in boiling water in a saucepan until just tender, about 7 minutes. Drain, return to pan, and immediately sprinkle with cheese and French dressing. Toss with a fork until cheese is melted, then cool. Add remaining ingredients except lettuce, toss to blend, then chill. Spoon onto lettuce to serve.

Serves 2.

# CHICKEN AND MELON SALAD 🐛🐛

| | |
|---|---|
| 1 cup | bite-size pieces cooked chicken |
| ½ cup | halved seedless green grapes |
| ¼ cup | sliced celery |
| 2 tbsp. | toasted slivered almonds |
| ¼ cup | light mayonnaise |
| ¼ tsp. | curry powder |
| Pinch | salt |
| ½ tsp. | soya sauce |
| 1 | small cantaloupe |
| | Lettuce |
| 1 tbsp. | toasted slivered almonds |

Combine chicken, grapes, celery, and 2 tbsp. almonds. Mix mayonnaise, curry powder, salt, and soya sauce. Add to chicken mixture and toss lightly. Chill.

Cut melon in half and discard seeds. Set melon on lettuce on serving plates and fill with chicken mixture. Sprinkle with the 1 tbsp. almonds. Serve immediately.

Serves 2.

## COLESLAW 🐛

| 3 cups | finely shredded cabbage (¼ medium) |
| --- | --- |
| 2 tsp. | sugar |
| ¾ tsp. | grated onion |
| 2 tsp. | white vinegar |
| ¼ cup | light cream |
| 2 tsp. | salad dressing or mayonnaise |
| ¼ tsp. | salt |
| ¼ tsp. | dry mustard |
| ½ tsp. | celery seed |

Put cabbage into a bowl. Combine remaining ingredients in a small jar with a tight lid and shake to blend well. Pour over cabbage and toss with a fork.

Serves 2.

## CABBAGE-APPLE SLAW 🍎

| | |
|---|---|
| 2 cups | finely shredded cabbage |
| ½ cup | chopped unpeeled apple |
| ¼ cup | broken walnuts |
| ½ tsp. | grated onion |
| 1 tbsp. | white vinegar |
| ½ tsp. | sugar |
| ¼ cup | light cream |
| 1 tbsp. | mayonnaise |
| ¼ tsp. | dry mustard |
| Pinch | salt |
| Dash | pepper |

Combine cabbage, apple, walnuts, and onion in a bowl. Put remaining ingredients in a small jar with a tight lid and shake to blend well. Pour over cabbage mixture and toss lightly. Chill until serving time.

Serves 2.

## GREEN AND RED CABBAGE SLAW ❦

| | |
|---|---|
| 1 cup | finely shredded savoy or other green cabbage |
| 1 cup | finely shredded red cabbage |
| ½ cup | diced celery |
| 2 tbsp. | finely chopped onion |
| 2 tbsp. | mayonnaise |
| 1½ tsp. | lemon juice |
| ¼ tsp. | salt |
| Dash | pepper |

Put cabbage, celery, and onion in a salad bowl. Mix mayonnaise, lemon juice, salt, and pepper and pour over vegetables. Toss lightly.

Serves 2.

## LETTUCE-PICKLE SLAW ❦

| | |
|---|---|
| ½ medium head | iceberg lettuce |
| ¼ cup | light mayonnaise |
| ⅓ cup | undrained sweet pickle relish |
| ⅛ tsp. | seasoned salt |
| Dash | black pepper |

Slice lettuce coarsely shortly before serving time. Put in a bowl. Combine remaining ingredients and pour over lettuce, then toss and serve as soon as possible.

Serves 2.

# BASIC FRENCH DRESSING ❦

| ½ cup | olive or salad oil |
| 2 tbsp. | vinegar |
| 2 tbsp. | lemon juice |
| ¼ tsp. | salt |
| ¼ tsp. | dry mustard |
| ¼ tsp. | paprika |

Shake all ingredients together in a small jar with a tight lid. Keep in refrigerator. Shake before using.

Makes about ¾ cup.

**Garlic French Dressing:** Let 1 clove garlic, cut in half, stand in the **Basic French Dressing** for at least 1 hour before using. When flavor is strong enough, discard garlic.

# TARRAGON FRENCH DRESSING ❦

| ¼ cup | red wine vinegar |
| Pinch | salt |
| Dash | pepper |
| ¾ cup | olive oil |
| ⅛ tsp. | dried leaf tarragon |

Combine ingredients in a jar with a tight lid and shake to blend. Let stand for at least 1 hour, then shake again before adding to salad.

Makes about 1 cup.

## SESAME DRESSING 🦗

| | |
|---|---|
| ⅓ cup | olive oil |
| 1 clove | garlic, peeled and cut in half |
| 1 tbsp. | sesame seeds |
| 2 tbsp. | wine vinegar |
| ¼ tsp. | salt |
| Dash | pepper |

Heat oil in small skillet. Add garlic and sesame seeds and heat gently, stirring until seeds are lightly browned. Discard garlic. Cool seeds.

Put seeds and oil in a small jar with a tight lid, add remaining ingredients and shake to blend well.

Makes ½ cup.

## CITRUS-PEANUT DRESSING 🦗

*Good for lettuce or fruit salads*

| | |
|---|---|
| ¼ tsp. | prepared mustard |
| ¼ cup | smooth peanut butter |
| 2 tbsp. | orange juice |
| ½ cup | plain yogurt |
| ½ tsp. | grated orange rind |

Blend mustard and peanut butter, then gradually beat in orange juice. Stir in yogurt and orange rind and beat until blended and smooth. Chill until needed.

Makes ¾ cup.

## SWEET BOILED DRESSING ❦❦

*For leaf lettuce, Waldorf, and fruit salads*

| | |
|---|---|
| 1 | egg |
| ¼ cup | sugar |
| 1½ tbsp. | flour |
| 1½ tsp. | dry mustard |
| Pinch | salt |
| ⅓ cup | white vinegar |
| 1 cup | milk |

Put egg, sugar, flour, mustard, and salt in a saucepan and beat with a wooden spoon until smooth. Stir in vinegar and milk.

Set over medium heat and cook, stirring constantly, until boiling. Boil 1 minute, stirring. Cool and store in refrigerator in a covered jar.

Makes 1½ cups.

**Note:** This keeps well in the refrigerator for several weeks.

## BLENDER MAYONNAISE 🦌🦌

| | |
|---|---|
| 1 | egg |
| ¼ tsp. | salt |
| ½ tsp. | dry mustard |
| ¼ tsp. | paprika (optional) |
| 2 tbsp. | white vinegar |
| 1 cup | oil (olive oil, salad oil, or a mixture of the two) |

Put egg, salt, mustard, paprika, vinegar, and ¼ cup of the oil into the blender. Cover and blend at high speed for a few seconds. Remove feeder cap and pour in the remaining oil in a thin, steady stream. Turn off the motor as soon as the oil has been added and the mixture has thickened. If you see the blender is not mixing in the last of the oil, turn off the machine and give the mayonnaise a final stir with a rubber scraper.

Makes about 1¼ cups.

**Note:** If you like a mild-flavored mayonnaise, reduce vinegar to 2 tsp. or use lemon juice in place of vinegar.

# COOKING TIMES FOR COMMON VEGETABLES

(Microwave times are for 2 servings at high. Allow 2 minutes standing time.)

| Vegetable | Preparation | MINUTES Simmer-ing | Steaming | Micro-wave |
|---|---|---|---|---|
| **Asparagus** | Spears | 8 to 10 | About 8 | About 4 |
| **Beans (green and yellow)** | 1-inch pieces | 10 to 15 | 10 to 12 | About 7 |
| **Beans** | Frenched | 5 to 7 | About 5 | |
| **Beets** | Whole (medium) | 40 to 50 (boiling) | | |
| **Broccoli** | Spears | 7 to 12 | About 10 | About 5 |
| **Brussels sprouts** | Whole | 8 to 10 | 15 to 20 | About 3½ |
| **Cabbage** | Wedges | 10 to 15 | About 20 | 6 to 7 |
| **Carrots** | Slices or strips | 10 to 15 | About 10 | 5 to 6 |
| **Cauliflower** | Flowerets | 10 to 12 | About 6 | About 6 |
| **Parsnips** | Sliced | 15 to 20 | 10 to 12 | 5 to 6 |
| **Peas** | Shelled | About 5 | 5 to 7 | About 5 |
| **Rutabagas** | Cubes | About 20 | About 25 | 7 to 10 |
| **Spinach** | Stems removed | 3 | | |
| **Squash (summer)** | Cubes or slices | 7 to 8 | About 7 | About 5 |

**Potatoes:** To bake, scrub and prick with a fork, then put in a 375 °F oven and bake about 1 hour or until tender. To boil, scrub and cook with skin on or thinly peeled. Cover with boiling water, return to a boil, reduce heat but continue boiling until tender, about 20 minutes for halves or quarters. To microwave, scrub, prick, and arrange in a circle in microwave oven. Microwave at high for about 12 minutes or until tender. Let stand 1 minute.

**Winter Squash:** To bake (small hubbard, acorn, or butternut), cut squash in half, do not remove seeds, and put cut side down on greased cookie sheet or baking dish. Bake in 350 °F oven until it starts to get tender, about 30 minutes. Turn and scoop out seeds and discard. Add a bit of butter, some salt and pepper, and a little brown sugar, if you like, to each piece of squash and continue baking until tender, 15 to 30 minutes more.

**Corn:** To boil, put husked corn in boiling unsalted water to cover, bring back to boil, and boil uncovered about 5 minutes or until very tender. To microwave, husk and wrap each cob in transparent wrap, twisting ends. Cook at high 2½ to 3 minutes for each ear, turning once. Let stand, wrapped 1 minute.

**To cream cooked vegetables**: Add 2 cups cooked vegetables to 1 cup **White Sauce** (page 76).

**To scallop cooked vegetables**: Turn creamed vegetables into a small casserole and top with ½ cup fine, dry bread crumbs or cracker crumbs mixed with 2 tbsp. melted butter or margarine. Bake at 350 °F for about 20 minutes or until bubbling and top is browned.

**For au gratin cooked vegetables**: Prepare as for scalloped except add ½ cup grated cheddar cheese to the fine, dry bread crumbs and melted butter.

## HERBED LIMA BEANS 🐢

| | |
|---|---|
| 2 tbsp. | cooking oil |
| 1 | small onion, chopped finely |
| 1 clove | garlic, chopped finely |
| 1 cup | canned tomatoes with juice |
| ½ tsp. | dried leaf marjoram |
| 12-oz. pkg. | frozen lima beans |
| 1 tbsp. | chopped parsley |
| ¼ tsp. | salt |
| ⅛ tsp. | pepper |

Heat oil in medium saucepan, add onion and garlic, and cook gently 3 minutes. Chop any large pieces of tomato and add the tomatoes and their liquid to the saucepan. Add marjoram, cover, and simmer 2 minutes. Add lima beans, cover, and cook 12 minutes or until beans are tender. Sprinkle in remaining ingredients and stir lightly to blend. Serve in individual dishes.

Makes 4 servings.

# FRESH ASPARAGUS ❦

| 1 lb. | fresh asparagus |
|---|---|
| | Butter |
| | Salt |
| | Pepper |

Choose asparagus stalks that are straight, green, and brittle with close, compact scales at the tips. Break off each stalk as far down as it snaps easily. Save about 4 of these tough bottoms and discard the rest. Remove scales from asparagus stalks with a sharp knife or vegetable peeler if they have collected sand. Wash asparagus well. If some stalks are very large, split the thick ends up about 1 inch.

Lay the tough ends you saved in a skillet in a straight line across the pan toward the side away from the handle. Lay the prepared asparagus stalks close together in a row, with the tips resting on the tough ends so the tips are raised out of the water and the lower parts of the stalks are in the water. (Arranging the stalks this way means the tips will steam while the lower ends boil.) Add about ½ inch boiling water to the pan, cover, and cook about 5 minutes for thin stalks and 8 to 10 minutes for thick stalks, or just until the lower parts of the stalks are barely tender. Drain. Pour a little melted butter over the asparagus and sprinkle lightly with salt and pepper. Serve immediately. (Discard the tough ends you used to support the tips.)

Serves 2.

**To Microwave:** Put ¼ cup water in an oblong baking dish, about 10 x 6 x 2 inches. Add asparagus, putting thick ends toward outside of dish and tips toward center. Cover with plastic wrap and turn back one corner to vent. Microwave at medium about 4 minutes, turning ½ turn after 2 minutes.

## QUICK MUSTARD-BEAN PICKLES 🦌🦌

| | |
|---|---|
| 14-oz. can | cut yellow beans |
| 1½ tbsp. | dry mustard |
| 1 tbsp. | flour |
| ¼ cup | sugar |
| ¼ tsp. | salt |
| ¼ tsp. | turmeric |
| ¼ cup | water (drained from beans) |
| ½ cup | white vinegar |
| ½ tsp. | celery seeds |

Drain beans, saving ¼ cup of the liquid. Combine mustard, flour, sugar, salt, and turmeric in a small bowl, then gradually stir in the water saved from the beans to make a smooth paste.

Heat vinegar and celery seed to boiling. Gradually add about ¼ cup of this mixture to mustard mixture, then stir this mixture gradually back into the boiling vinegar. Cook over medium heat, stirring constantly, 5 minutes. Add beans and bring to a boil. Ladle into sterilized jars and seal.

Makes about 2 cups.

## ZESTY BEANS 🐞🐞

| | |
|---|---|
| 3 strips | bacon |
| 10-oz. pkg. | frozen cut green beans |
| | Water |
| 1 tbsp. | flour |
| ⅔ cup | liquid (bean cooking liquid plus water) |
| 1 tbsp. | white vinegar |
| 1 tsp. | sugar |
| 1 tsp. | prepared mustard |
| ¼ tsp. | salt |
| ⅛ tsp. | pepper |

Fry bacon in skillet, lift out, cool, and crumble. Drain all but 1 tbsp. fat from pan.

Cook beans until tender-crisp, about 5 minutes. Drain, saving cooking liquid. Add water to cooking liquid to make the ⅔ cup liquid called for.

Stir flour into fat in pan, remove from heat, and stir in the ⅔ cup liquid, vinegar, sugar, mustard, salt, and pepper. Return to heat and cook, stirring until thick and smooth. Add beans and heat well. Sprinkle with bacon bits and serve immediately.

Serves 2 or 3.

# ORANGE BEETS 🐦

| | |
|---|---|
| 1 tsp. | cornstarch |
| ⅔ cup | orange juice |
| 1 tsp. | butter |
| 1 tbsp. | liquid honey |
| Pinch | salt |
| Dash | pepper |
| 1½ cups | diced cooked beets (canned are fine) |
| 1 tsp. | grated orange rind |

Blend cornstarch into orange juice in a small saucepan. Bring to a boil over high heat, stirring. Stir in butter, honey, salt, and pepper. Turn heat to low and stir 2 minutes. Add beets and heat well. Sprinkle with orange rind.

Serves 2.

# BUTTER-STEAMED BROCCOLI 🍂🍂

| ¾ lb. (approx.) | broccoli |
| --- | --- |
| 1½ tbsp. | butter or margarine |
| 4 tbsp. | water |
| ¼ tsp. | salt |
| Dash | pepper |
| ½ pkg. (125 g) | cream cheese, cubed |
| 1½ tsp. | lemon juice |

Wash broccoli, cut off flower ends, and set them aside. Cut away any tough stem ends and cut remaining stems into slices ⅛ inch thick.

Heat butter or margarine in electric skillet set at highest heat or in a heavy skillet set over high heat just until it begins to brown slightly. Add broccoli stems and stir. Add 2 tbsp. of the water, cover tightly, and cook 4 minutes, stirring several times. Add broccoli flowers and the remaining 2 tbsp. water, cover again, and continue cooking about 3 minutes, stirring several times. Cook just until broccoli is tender-crisp and water has evaporated. Turn off heat, sprinkle broccoli with salt and pepper, and add cubes of cheese. Stir gently just until cheese melts. Sprinkle in lemon juice and serve immediately.

Serves 2.

# SWEET-SOUR RED CABBAGE ❦

| | |
|---|---|
| 1 tbsp. | bacon drippings or vegetable oil |
| 2 cups | shredded red cabbage |
| 1 cup | small cubes peeled apple (1 medium) |
| 1 tbsp. | brown sugar |
| 2 tbsp. | white vinegar |
| 2 tbsp. | water |
| ¼ tsp. | salt |
| Dash | pepper |
| ¼ tsp. | caraway seeds |

Heat bacon drippings or oil in a skillet. Add cabbage and apple. Combine remaining ingredients and pour over cabbage mixture. Cover tightly and cook over low heat, stirring occasionally, 20 minutes or until cabbage is tender. Serve immediately.

Serves 2.

**To Microwave:** Put cabbage in 1½ quart casserole. Add bacon drippings or oil, apple, vinegar, and water. Cover and cook at high 5 minutes, until cabbage and apple are tender, stirring after 3 minutes. Stir in brown sugar, salt, pepper, and caraway seeds. Cover and cook 2 minutes or until liquid is bubbling.

## SAVORY CARROTS ❧

| | |
|---|---|
| 1½ cups | sliced carrots |
| ⅛ tsp. | salt |
| 2 tsp. | butter or margarine |
| 2 tsp. | chopped onion |
| 2 tbsp. | chopped green pepper |
| | Salt and pepper |

Put carrots in a medium saucepan with ⅛ tsp. salt and a small amount of water. Cover and cook 5 minutes. Drain and push carrots to one side of pan. Add butter or margarine to other side of pan, add onion and green pepper to butter or margarine and stir over low heat 1 minute. Stir carrots and onion-green pepper mixture together, season lightly, cover, and continue cooking over low heat, stirring occasionally, until everything is tender, about 5 minutes.

Serves 2.

## GLAZED BABY CARROTS 🐝

| | |
|---|---|
| ½ lb. | small carrots |
| 1 tbsp. | butter or margarine |
| 1 tsp. | sugar |
| Dash | salt |
| Dash | pepper |
| 1 tsp. | finely chopped fresh mint |

Scrub and trim carrots. Cook whole in a small amount of boiling water until tender. Drain. Add remaining ingredients except mint and shake over high heat to coat carrots with butter-sugar mixture. Turn heat to low and shake until carrots are glazed, about 3 minutes. Sprinkle with mint and serve immediately.

Serves 2.

**Note:** If tiny new carrots aren't available, cut large carrots into strips about pencil-size in diameter.

## CUCUMBER WITH MINT 🌿🌿

| ½ slice | day-old white bread |
| 1 tsp. | butter or margarine |
| 2 | medium cucumbers |
| 1 tbsp. | butter or margarine |
| 1 tbsp. | finely chopped fresh mint leaves |
| | Salt and pepper |

Cut crusts from bread and cut bread into ¼-inch cubes. Heat the 1 tsp. butter or margarine in a small skillet over medium heat, add bread cubes, and stir until golden and crisp. Set aside.

Peel cucumbers, cut in quarters lengthwise, and seed. Cut into 1-inch pieces. Heat the 1 tbsp. butter or margarine in a skillet over medium heat. Add cucumber pieces and mint and sprinkle lightly with salt and pepper. Cover and cook over low heat, shaking pan often, until just tender, about 7 minutes. Turn into serving bowl, sprinkle with crisp bread cubes and serve immediately.

Serves 2.

## SCALLOPED POTATOES 🐛🐛

| | |
|---|---|
| 4 | medium potatoes |
| 2 tbsp. | finely chopped parsley |
| ¼ cup | chopped onion |
| | Salt and pepper |
| 1 tbsp. | butter or margarine |
| 1½ cups | hot milk (approximately) |

Heat oven to 350 °F. Butter a 1-qt. casserole.

Peel potatoes and grate on coarse grater (but do not grate until ready to use them). Combine parsley and onion. Put a thick layer of the grated potato in the casserole, sprinkle with salt and pepper and dot lightly with butter. Sprinkle with some of the parsley-onion mixture. Repeat until ingredients are all used, ending with a potato layer. Dot with butter and add enough milk to nearly cover the potatoes, then bake, uncovered, until potatoes are tender and milk is absorbed, for about 1¼ hours.

Serves 2.

### Potatoes Boulangère

Prepare as for **Scalloped Potatoes** except slice potatoes thinly and replace milk with water.

**To Microwave:** Cook at high, covered, until potatoes are tender, about 10 minutes. Stir several times during cooking. Let stand, covered, 10 minutes, then serve.

## PEAS IN CREAM 🐢

| | |
|---|---|
| 1½ cups | frozen peas |
| 1 tsp. | sugar |
| 2 | green onions with tops, sliced thin |
| ¼ cup | boiling water |
| 1 tsp. | butter or margarine |
| ¼ tsp. | salt |
| Dash | pepper |
| ¼ cup | light cream |

Combine peas, sugar, and onions in a small saucepan. Add water, cover, and bring to a boil. Reduce heat and boil gently 3 minutes. Do not drain. Add butter or margarine and heat until melted. Add salt, pepper, and cream. Heat but do not boil. Serve immediately in individual dishes.

Serves 2.

## BROILED TOMATOES 🐛

| 2 | medium tomatoes |
| | Salt and pepper |
| | Dried leaf chervil or basil |
| 3 tbsp. | fine, dry bread crumbs |
| 2 tsp. | melted butter or margarine |

Cut each tomato in half, crosswise. Sprinkle with salt and pepper and lightly with chervil or basil. Combine bread crumbs and melted butter or margarine and sprinkle thickly on top of each slice of tomato, patting down lightly. Put on broiler pan and broil about 6 inches from heat until topping is lightly browned and tomatoes are warm.

Serves 2.

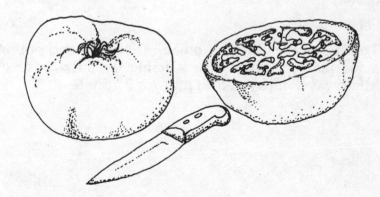

## BAKED TOMATOES ❦

| | |
|---|---|
| 2 | medium tomatoes |
| | Salt and pepper |
| | Dried leaf oregano |
| 1 tbsp. | butter or margarine |
| 2 tbsp. | fine, dry bread crumbs |
| 1 tbsp. | grated Parmesan cheese |

Cut tops and a small sliver from the bottoms of the tomatoes and put them in a small, buttered baking dish. Sprinkle lightly with salt and pepper and add a pinch of oregano to each. Melt butter or margarine in a small saucepan, remove from heat, and blend in crumbs and cheese. Mix well and put half of mixture in a thick layer on top of each tomato.

Heat oven to 450°F shortly before serving time. Bake tomatoes about 10 minutes or until hot and topping is browned.

Serves 2.

**To Microwave:** Prepare tomatoes as above and put on a pie plate or other dish suitable for microwaving. Microwave, uncovered, at high for 3 minutes.

# SCALLOPED TOMATOES ❦❦

| | |
|---|---|
| 1 tbsp. | butter or margarine |
| ⅓ cup | chopped celery |
| 3 tbsp. | finely chopped onion |
| 1 tbsp. | flour |
| 14-oz. can | tomatoes |
| 1 tsp. | sugar |
| ½ tsp. | salt |
| ¼ tsp. | pepper |
| 1 tsp. | prepared mustard |
| 2 slices | day-old bread, toasted lightly and buttered |
| | Grated Parmesan or cheddar cheese |

Heat butter or margarine in a medium saucepan. Add celery and onion and cook gently 3 minutes. Sprinkle in flour and stir to blend. Remove from heat and stir in tomatoes (cut them up if they are whole), sugar, salt, pepper, and mustard. Bring to a boil.

Heat oven to 350°F. Butter a 1-qt. casserole. Cut toast in 1-inch squares.

Pour about a third of the tomato mixture into the prepared casserole. Top with half the toast squares. Add another third of the tomato mixture and remaining toast squares. End with a final layer of the tomato mixture and a sprinkling of cheese (2 or 3 tbsp.). Bake 20 minutes or until very hot.

Serves 2.

## BUTTER-STEAMED ZUCCHINI ❧

| | |
|---|---|
| 2 tbsp. | butter or margarine |
| 2 | small zucchini, sliced thin |
| ¼ cup | water |
| | Pepper |
| 2 tbsp. | grated Parmesan cheese |

Melt butter or margarine in a small skillet. Add zucchini and water and cook 2 minutes, shaking the pan often. Sprinkle lightly with pepper and then with cheese. Cover and heat 30 seconds to melt cheese. Serve immediately.

Serves 2.

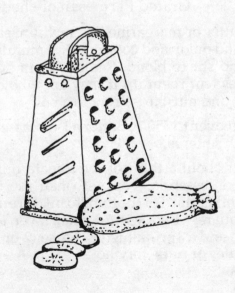

## PLAIN-FRIED VEGETABLES 🐞🐞

| | |
|---|---|
| 4 | large stalks celery |
| 2 | medium onions |
| ½ | large green pepper |
| 2 tbsp. | water |
| 1 tsp. | cornstarch |
| 2 tbsp. | peanut or other vegetable oil |
| 2 tsp. | soya sauce |
| ¼ cup | water |

Cut celery in ¼-inch slices on the diagonal. Cut onions in half lengthwise and lay on board, cut side down. Slice paper thin. Cut pepper in thin strips lengthwise. Mix 2 tbsp. water and cornstarch, blending until smooth.

Heat oil in large heavy skillet or wok until very hot. Add celery and cook over high heat 30 seconds, stirring constantly. Add onions and cook and stir 30 seconds. Add green pepper and cook and stir another 30 seconds. Add soya sauce and ¼ cup water, cover, turn heat to medium, and simmer 2 minutes.

Shove vegetables to one side of pan and stir enough of the cornstarch mixture into the boiling liquid to make a sauce thick enough to cling to the vegetables. Stir all together and serve immediately.

Serves 2 generously.

**Note:** This is a good basic way of cooking almost any vegetable or combination of vegetables. If you are using several vegetables, add them in order as I have here — with those that take the longest cooking time first.

# BAKED BARLEY AND MUSHROOMS ❦

| | |
|---|---|
| ½ cup | pot barley |
| 1 cup | hot chicken stock (or 1 chicken bouillon cube dissolved in 1 cup boiling water) |
| 1 tbsp. | butter or margarine |
| ½ cup | sliced fresh mushrooms |
| 2 tsp. | chopped parsley |
| | Salt and pepper to taste |

Heat oven to 325°F. Combine barley and half the stock in a small casserole (20-oz. size is good). Cover tightly and bake 30 minutes. Stir with a fork and add remaining stock, then cover tightly again and bake until barley is tender, about 30 minutes more.

Shortly before barley is done, heat butter or margarine in a small skillet over high heat and fry mushrooms until lightly browned, about 3 minutes. Add to cooked barley along with parsley, salt, and pepper. Toss with a fork and serve.

Serves 2.

**Note:** A nice variation of this recipe is to use 1 medium green pepper cut in ½-inch squares in place of or in addition to mushrooms.

## BAKED BROWN RICE 🦃

| | |
|---|---|
| 1 tbsp. | butter or margarine |
| ½ cup | chopped onion (1 medium) |
| ½ cup | chopped celery |
| ¾ cup | uncooked brown rice |
| 1¾ cups | chicken stock (page 64) or water |
| ½ tsp. | salt |
| | Dash black pepper |

Heat oven to 375 °F. Butter a 1-qt. casserole.

Melt butter or margarine in a medium saucepan over medium heat. Add onion and celery and stir 5 minutes. Mix in rice, chicken stock or water, salt, and pepper. Bring to a boil. Pour into prepared casserole, cover, and bake 45 minutes. Uncover, stir lightly with a fork, and continue baking, uncovered, until liquid is absorbed but rice is still moist, about 10 minutes.

Makes 3 or 4 servings.

# FRUITED RICE ❦❦

| 2 tsp. | cooking oil |
| --- | --- |
| ⅓ cup | sliced green onions |
| ⅓ cup | thinly sliced carrot |
| ⅔ cup | chopped unpeeled apple |
| 3 tbsp. | finely chopped dried apricots |
| 3 tbsp. | seedless raisins |
| 1 cup | cooked brown rice (page 33) |
| ¼ tsp. | salt |
| Pinch | dried leaf savory |
| 1 tsp. | toasted sesame seeds (optional) |

Heat oil in a medium saucepan over medium heat. Add onions and carrot and stir constantly 5 minutes. Add apple, apricots, and raisins and stir 10 minutes. Stir in rice, salt, and savory. Cover and heat gently until rice is hot, stirring lightly with a fork several times. Sprinkle with sesame seeds. Good with chicken dishes and curries.

Serves 2 or 3.

# BREADS AND CEREALS

# BREADS AND CEREALS

Whole grain and enriched breads and cereals provide carbohydrates (starch and sugar for energy and fiber for bulk), iron and B vitamins (for maintenance of a healthy nervous system and digestive tract, healthy skin and eyes, and, in the case of iron, an essential part of hemoglobin), and a limited source of protein (for tissue repair and to help fight infections). Since all white flour is enriched with iron, thiamin, riboflavin, and niacin, these nutrients are in all homemade and commercial baked things.

Because breads and cereals provide all these good things (most breakfast cereals and pastas are also enriched with B vitamins), it's important to include them in your everyday meals even if you are watching calories. Just remember that cakes, cookies, pastries, doughnuts, etc., while made with enriched flour or even whole wheat flour, also give you a lot of added fat and sugar, so it is wise to avoid them as much as possible.

Brown and parboiled or converted rice are good bets. Both have more thiamin and iron than unenriched white rice and brown rice also has more niacin.

If you've never tried making yeast bread, you should — just for the fun of it! The **No-Knead Oatmeal Bread** recipe in this section is a particularly good one for beginners (but you experts — it's too good to pass up!) since it is just mixed and put into the pans to rise. I'm sure it will encourage beginners to try other bread recipes. There are also recipes here for corn bread, biscuits, muffins, pancakes, waffles, French toast, and a choice of sandwiches, as well as two unusual ways to prepare hot cereal.

## NO-KNEAD OATMEAL BREAD 🦌🦌

| | |
|---|---|
| ¾ cup | boiling water |
| ½ cup | quick-cooking rolled oats |
| 3 tbsp. | soft shortening |
| ¼ cup | liquid honey |
| 1 tsp. | salt |
| 1 tsp. | sugar |
| ¼ cup | warm water |
| 1 package | dry yeast |
| 1 | egg |
| ½ tsp. | ground nutmeg |
| 1 cup | whole wheat flour |
| ¼ cup | skim milk powder |
| 1 cup | sifted all-purpose flour |
| 1 tbsp. | quick-cooking rolled oats |

Combine boiling water, ½ cup rolled oats, shortening, honey, and salt in a large bowl. Stir to blend, then cool to lukewarm.

Grease 2 small (5¾ x 3¼ x 2-inch) foil loaf pans. Stir sugar into ¼ cup warm water until dissolved, then sprinkle yeast over water and let stand 10 minutes. Stir well.

Beat egg lightly with a fork, measure out 2 tsp., and set aside. Add remaining egg to rolled oats mixture along with yeast mixture, nutmeg, whole wheat flour, skim milk powder, and half the all-purpose flour. Beat hard with a wooden spoon for 2 minutes, scraping the sides and bottom of the bowl often. Add remaining flour and mix well. Dough will be soft.

Divide dough in two and put half in each of the prepared pans. Pat with a floured hand to level top. Cover with a damp cloth and let rise in a warm place until dough is almost at the top of the pans, about 1½ hours.

Heat oven to 375°F. Brush top of dough with reserved 2 tsp. egg and sprinkle with the 1 tbsp. rolled oats. Bake until loaves sound hollow when tapped on top, about 30 minutes. Turn out of pans and cool on rack.

Makes 2 small loaves, one for today, the other to freeze.

**Note:** If you find the loaves are browning too much, cover loosely with foil.

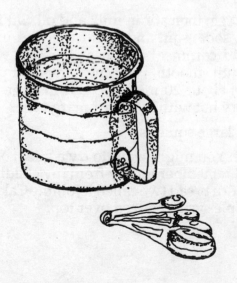

## CORN BREAD 🐦

| 1 | egg |
|---|---|
| 1½ cups | buttermilk |
| ¼ cup | cooking oil |
| ½ cup | sifted all-purpose flour |
| 1 tbsp. | baking powder |
| ½ tsp. | baking soda |
| ½ tsp. | salt |
| 1 tsp. | sugar |
| 1½ cups | cornmeal |
| | Butter or margarine |

Heat oven to 450°F. Grease an 8-inch square cake pan generously. Put it in the oven to heat while mixing batter.

Beat egg, then stir in milk and oil. Sift flour, baking powder, soda, salt, and sugar together into first mixture. Add cornmeal and beat together with a rotary beater until smooth. Pour into prepared pan and bake until set, about 20 minutes. Cut in large squares and serve very hot with butter or margarine.

Makes 4 large squares.

**Note:** You might want to try a good, old-fashioned dessert I remember fondly from my childhood in Winnipeg: Corn Bread (we called it Johnny Cake) served hot with maple syrup poured over top.

# REFRIGERATOR BRAN MUFFINS ❦

| | |
|---|---|
| 3 cups | All Bran cereal |
| 1 cup | boiling water |
| ½ cup | cooking oil |
| ½ cup | molasses |
| 2 | eggs |
| 2 cups | buttermilk |
| 1 cup | uncooked cut-up prunes |
| 2½ cups | sifted all-purpose flour |
| 1 tbsp. | baking soda |
| ½ tsp. | salt |

Mix cereal with boiling water in a large bowl and let stand until cool. Pour oil into a 2-cup measure or bowl. Add molasses, then eggs, and beat with a fork. Stir egg mixture into bran along with buttermilk and prunes. Sift flour, soda, and salt together into bran mixture and stir just to blend. Refrigerate in a tightly covered container.

Bake these muffins as you need them. The batter will keep at least 2 weeks if covered and refrigerated.

When you want fresh muffins, heat oven to 425°F and grease as many large muffin cups as you need. Spoon in batter, filling two-thirds full. Bake about 15 minutes or until done. Serve warm.

The whole recipe makes about 2 dozen large muffins.

## BASIC BISCUIT MIX 🍂

| | |
|---|---|
| 6 cups | sifted all-purpose flour |
| ¼ cup | baking powder |
| 2 tsp. | salt |
| 1½ cups | solid vegetable shortening |

Sift flour, baking powder, and salt into a large bowl. Add shortening and cut in finely with a pastry blender or two knives (one in each hand, cutting against each other). Mix well with a fork before using in any of the recipes in this section. (See **Tea Biscuits,** page 175; **Muffins,** page 176; **Pancakes,** page 178; **Waffles,** page 178; **Coffee Cake,** page 181; and **Steak Pie,** page 86.)

**Note:** Double the recipe if you intend to make use of the mix often. If you use vegetable shortening and store the mixture in a tight glass or plastic container, it will stay fresh at room temperature for a month or more. Or, if you prefer, you can divide it into 1-cup measures in small freezer bags and store them in the freezer for up to 6 months.

# TEA BISCUITS 🐦

⅓ cup       milk

1 cup       Basic Biscuit Mix (page 174)

Heat oven to 450 °F. Have ready ungreased cookie sheet.

Add milk to biscuit mix in a bowl and stir briskly with a fork just until blended, about 12 strokes. Turn out on floured board and knead 10 times. (Instructions for how to knead are given on page 14.) Shape into a round and pat or roll to ½-inch thick. Cut into wedges or with a biscuit cutter. Put on cookie sheet and bake 8 to 10 minutes until well browned.

Makes 6 medium biscuits.

# MUFFINS 🐾

| 1 | egg |
|---|---|
| ⅔ cup | milk |
| ¼ cup | sugar |
| 1½ cups | Basic Biscuit Mix (page 174) |

Heat oven to 400°F. Grease 6 large muffin cups or line them with paper baking cups.

Beat egg, milk, and sugar together with a fork. Stir in biscuit mix, using as few strokes as possible. Dry ingredients should be dampened but batter should still be a little lumpy. Spoon into prepared muffin cups and bake about 15 minutes or until tops spring back when touched lightly.

Makes 6.

**Note:** For variety, you may add ⅓ cup chopped nuts, dates, or apricots or ¼ cup seedless raisins to egg mixture.

# BLUEBERRY MUFFINS 🐾

Make as for **Muffins,** above, adding ½ tsp. grated lemon rind to the egg mixture and folding ½ cup frozen blueberries into batter at end of mixing. (Add the berries while still frozen, otherwise they will color the batter blue.)

## BRAN MUFFINS 🍎

| ¾ cup | milk |
|---|---|
| 1 | egg |
| 2 tbsp. | molasses |
| ½ cup | natural bran |
| ¼ cup | seedless raisins |
| 1 cup | Basic Biscuit Mix (page 174) |

Heat oven to 400 °F. Grease 8 large muffin cups.

Beat milk, egg, and molasses together with a fork. Stir in bran and raisins, then add biscuit mix, stirring as directed in **Muffins** recipe (page 176). Bake about 15 minutes.

Makes 8.

## PANCAKES ❦

| | |
|---|---|
| 1 cup | Basic Biscuit Mix (page 174) |
| 1 | egg |
| ¾ cup | milk |

Combine ingredients in a bowl and beat with a rotary beater until smooth. Use about ¼ cup of batter for each pancake and bake on hot greased skillet or griddle. As soon as bubbles appear on the surface of the baking pancakes, turn and bake on the other side until nicely browned.

Makes 8.

## WAFFLES ❦

Make batter as for **Pancakes** (above) except add 2 tbsp. melted shortening or cooking oil to the batter. Bake in hot waffle iron.

Makes 1 large.

## WHOLE WHEAT PANCAKES ❦ ❦

| | |
|---|---|
| 1 | egg |
| 1 tbsp. | cooking oil |
| ⅔ cup | water |
| ⅔ cup | whole wheat flour |
| 2 tbsp. | wheat germ |
| ⅓ cup | skim milk powder |
| 1 tsp. | baking powder |
| Dash | salt |
| | Hot applesauce (Use homemade, page 217, or commercial) |

Beat egg well with the oil, then beat in the water. Combine remaining ingredients except applesauce and add, beating well until smooth.

Bake batter on a hot, lightly greased griddle or skillet, using ¼ cup batter for each pancake and cooking just until bubbles form on the first side. Turn and cook until well browned on second side. Serve hot with hot applesauce spooned over.

Makes about 6 large.

## FRENCH TOAST 🐞

| 1 | egg |
| 1 tbsp. | maple syrup |
| 4 thick | slices day-old French bread |
| 1 tbsp. | butter or margarine |
| | Maple syrup |

Beat egg and 1 tbsp. maple syrup in a flat dish (a pie plate works well). Dip bread slices in the mixture to coat both sides. Heat butter or margarine in a skillet over medium heat and fry the bread slices until brown on both sides. Serve hot with syrup poured over top.

Serves 2.

## CINNAMON TOAST 🐞

| 1½ tbsp. | soft butter or margarine |
| 1 tbsp. | brown sugar |
| ½ tsp. | ground cinnamon |
| 2 slices | hot whole wheat toast |

Cream together butter or margarine, brown sugar, and cinnamon and spread on the toast.

Makes 2 slices toast.

## COFFEE CAKE 🐛🐛

| 2 cups | Basic Biscuit Mix (page 174) |
| 1/4 cup | brown sugar |
| 1/2 tsp. | ground cinnamon |
| 1/2 tsp. | ground nutmeg |
| 2/3 cup | milk |
| 2 | eggs |
| 1/4 cup | chopped walnuts |

Heat oven to 350°F. Grease an 8-inch square cake pan.

Combine biscuit mix, brown sugar, cinnamon, and nutmeg and take out 1/2 cup of the mixture. Set it aside.

Beat milk and eggs together and add to remaining dry mixture, stirring just to blend. Turn into prepared pan and spread evenly.

Add nuts to the 1/2 cup dry mixture and sprinkle this mixture over the batter.

Bake 20 to 25 minutes or until a toothpick stuck in the center comes out clean. Serve warm.

## WHEAT GERM COFFEE CAKE 🐛🐛

Make as for **Coffee Cake** (above) except add 2/3 cup toasted wheat germ to biscuit mix, sugar, and spice mixture.

## GRILLED CHEESE SANDWICHES 🦌

| 4 slices | whole wheat bread |
| | Old cheddar cheese |
| | Prepared mustard |
| | Butter or margarine |

Cover 2 of the bread slices with slices of cheese. Spread the other 2 slices lightly with mustard. Top the cheese with these bread slices, mustard side in. Spread one side of each sandwich with butter or margarine. Heat a heavy skillet and put the sandwiches in the skillet, buttered side down. Butter second side of sandwiches. Brown both sides over medium heat. Cut in quarters to serve. Serve hot.

Makes 2.

## COUNTRY COTTAGE SANDWICHES 🦌

| ½ cup | drained cream-style cottage cheese |
| 2 tbsp. | finely chopped celery |
| 2 tbsp. | finely chopped radishes |
| 2 tsp. | finely chopped parsley |
| 2 tsp. | mayonnaise |
| | Dash pepper |
| 4 slices | rye bread, buttered |

Mash cottage cheese with a fork in a small dish until nearly smooth. Stir in remaining ingredients except bread. Spread filling between bread slices and cut each sandwich into fingers or small triangles.

Serves 2.

## PUFFY TUNA SANDWICHES 🦌🦌

| | |
|---|---|
| 6½-oz. can | chunk light tuna, drained and flaked |
| 2 tbsp. | light mayonnaise |
| 2 tsp. | lemon juice |
| 4 slices | whole wheat bread |
| 1 | egg white |
| 2 tbsp. | light mayonnaise |
| | Dash cayenne |
| 1 tbsp. | chopped parsley |
| 2 tbsp. | finely chopped sweet pickle, drained |
| | Paprika |

Blend tuna, 2 tbsp. mayonnaise, and lemon juice well with a fork. Toast bread on one side under broiler, turn, and toast other side very lightly. Spread the toast with the tuna mixture.

Beat egg white until stiff, then fold in 2 tbsp. mayonnaise, cayenne, parsley, and pickle. Spread over tuna.

Put low under hot broiler and broil until tops of sandwiches are delicately browned and puffed. Sprinkle lightly with paprika and serve immediately.

Makes 4 open-face sandwiches.

## TOASTED TOMATO CHEESIES ❦

| | |
|---|---|
| 4 slices | bacon, cut in half |
| 2 | English muffins |
| 4 | process cheese slices |
| 1 tbsp. | finely chopped onion |
| ½ tsp. | Worcestershire sauce |
| 1 | large tomato, cut into 4 thick slices |

Cook bacon until crisp, drain on paper towelling, and keep warm. Heat broiler.

Pry muffins apart with the tines of a fork and lay them, cut side down, on a cookie sheet. Slip muffins under the broiler and toast underside lightly. Remove from oven and turn muffins cut sides up. Top each with a slice of cheese. Combine onion and Worcestershire sauce and spread a small amount of this mixture on each cheese slice, then top with a tomato slice.

Return muffins to oven and broil until hot and bubbly. Slip 2 pieces of muffin onto each serving plate and garnish each with 2 pieces of bacon. Serve immediately.

Serves 2.

# WHOLE WHEAT RIBBONS 🍎

| | |
|---|---|
| ½ pkg.<br>(125 g) | cream cheese at room temperature |
| ½ tsp. | lemon juice |
| 2 tbsp. | finely chopped radishes |
| 1 tbsp. | finely chopped watercress leaves or parsley |
| ¼ tsp. | grated lemon rind |
| 4 | very thin slices whole wheat bread |

Blend cheese and lemon juice together, then stir in radishes, watercress or parsley, and lemon rind.

Cut crusts from bread and cut bread slices into strips 1-inch wide. Spread each strip with about 1½ tsp. of cheese mixture.

Makes 12 small open-face sandwiches.

## AVOCADO-TUNA PITA POCKETS 🦌🦌

| | |
|---|---|
| 1½ tbsp. | soft butter or margarine |
| ⅛ tsp. | Dijon mustard |
| ¼ cup | cream-style cottage cheese |
| 2 tbsp. | thinly sliced green onions |
| 2 tbsp. | finely chopped green pepper |
| 2 | pita breads, heated and cut in half crosswise |
| | Shredded lettuce |
| 1 | small avocado, sliced (see note) |
| 3¾-oz. can | solid tuna, drained and flaked |

Cream butter or margarine and mustard together. Combine cottage cheese, green onions, and green pepper.

Spread insides of pita pieces with mustard butter, then add some lettuce, some avocado slices, and a layer of tuna. Add about 1 tbsp. of the cottage cheese mixture to each half pita and spread it as much as possible. Serve immediately.

Makes 4 pita pockets.

**Note:** Whole wheat pitas are best and most supermarkets carry them in the bread section. Buy the ones that are about 6 inches in diameter for this recipe. To heat, wrap in foil, and heat 10 minutes at 400 °F. Don't peel and slice the avocado until you are ready to use it — otherwise it will turn dark.

# HAM AND SLAW PITA POCKETS 🐛🐛

| ½ cup | finely shredded cabbage |
|---|---|
| 1 tbsp. | finely chopped green pepper |
| 1 tbsp. | finely grated carrot |
| 1 tbsp. | light mayonnaise |
| Pinch | salt |
| Dash | pepper |
| Pinch | celery seeds (optional) |
| 2 | pita breads, heated and cut in half crosswise (see note on page 186) |
| | Soft butter or margarine |
| 2 slices | process cheese |
| 2 | thin slices cooked ham |
| 2 | large thin slices tomato |
| | Shredded lettuce |
| | Sweet pickles, sliced thin |

Combine first 7 ingredients and chill.

Spread insides of warm pita halves lightly with butter or margarine. Put a half slice of cheese in each half, then 2 tbsp. of the cabbage mixture, a half ham slice and a half tomato slice. Add some lettuce and a few slices of pickle. Serve immediately.

Makes 4 pita pockets.

## APPLE-FLAVORED HOT CEREAL 🐦

| 1½ cups | apple juice |
| ¼ cup | quick cream of wheat |
| 2 tbsp. | natural bran |
| ¼ tsp. | salt |
| ½ tsp. | ground cinnamon |
| ¼ cup | seedless raisins or chopped dates |
| | Brown sugar (optional) |
| | Milk |

Heat apple juice to a full rolling boil, then sprinkle in the cream of wheat gradually, stirring constantly. Add bran, salt, and cinnamon, bring back to a boil, reduce heat to low, and stir until mixture thickens, about 5 minutes. Stir in raisins or dates. Serve immediately, sprinkled lightly with brown sugar and with milk poured over all. (The apple juice makes the cereal quite sweet, so you may prefer not to add sugar.)

Serves 2.

## CREAMY BARLEY 🍎🍎

| 1¼ cups | water |
| 1⁄2 cup | barley flakes |
| 1⁄8 tsp. | salt |
| 2 | eggs |
| 2 tbsp. | brown sugar |
| 3⁄4 cup | milk |
| Pinch | salt |
| 1⁄4 cup | chopped uncooked prunes |
| 1⁄4 tsp. | vanilla extract |

Combine water, barley flakes, and 1⁄8 tsp. salt in a small saucepan. Bring to a boil, reduce heat, cover, and cook gently 10 minutes. Uncover and stir 5 minutes, then remove from heat.

Beat eggs, sugar, milk, and pinch salt with a wooden spoon in the top of a double boiler. Add prunes and cook over simmering water, stirring constantly, until mixture coats a metal spoon like a thin custard, about 10 minutes. Stir in vanilla and cooked barley flakes and heat well. Serve with milk as breakfast cereal.

Serves 2.

**Note:** You should be able to find barley flakes at a health food store.

# SWEETS

# SWEETS

I doubt any of us want to go through life avoiding all sweets. But the experts advise moderation and most of us realize that, while every now and then it's all right to splurge, we should stick to desserts that are good for us the rest of the time. And that's really not too hard to take.

Many of these recipes are fruit based. Fruit supplies all the goodness described on page 127 at the beginning of the Salads and Vegetables recipes. (Fruits supplying folic acid include avocados, cantaloupes, and oranges, and those supplying iron include dried apricots, dates, prunes, and raisins.)

When you look over these recipes, you may think I'm in the dairy business. A majority of them call for milk, yogurt, cottage cheese, cheese, etc. There's a good reason for that. Nutritionists worry about seniors because many people "beyond young" have given up drinking milk. Sometimes we think it's only good for children; sometimes we have difficulty digesting it. But we should be getting the goodness of milk products no matter what our age, mainly because they supply us with calcium (for preservation and repair of bones plus healthy nerve function and normal blood clotting). Dairy products also supply B vitamins and high quality protein. Vitamin A occurs naturally in whole milk, and 2% and skim milks are fortified with it. All milk sold in retail stores is fortified with Vitamin D (which helps in absorption of calcium and phosphorus).

By the way, don't count on whipping cream, sour cream, butter, or even cream cheese for your nutritional needs. They are not considered to be part of this essential group of foods because they are high in fat and contain very little calcium.

If you think you don't like yogurt (it's a very good way to get the advantages of milk because it's so easily digested), try **Easy Individual Trifles** on page 214, or **Kiwi and Banana** on page 220. I think you're in for a pleasant surprise.

# BUTTERSCOTCH-OAT SQUARES 🍎

| | |
|---|---|
| ¼ cup | butter or margarine |
| ⅔ cup | packed brown sugar |
| ½ tsp. | vanilla extract |
| 1 cup | quick-cooking rolled oats |
| ¼ cup | chopped walnuts |
| ¼ cup | sifted all-purpose flour |
| 1 tsp. | baking powder |
| ¼ tsp. | salt |

Heat oven to 300 °F. Grease an 8-inch square cake pan.

Melt butter or margarine in a medium saucepan. Stir in sugar, vanilla, rolled oats, and nuts. Sift flour, baking powder, and salt together into mixture and mix until blended, first with a spoon then with fingers. Turn into prepared pan and pat down evenly.

Bake until set, about 25 minutes. Let cool in pan 10 minutes, then cut into small squares. Finish cooling in pan.

# HONEY-PEANUT BUTTER COOKIES 🐾🐾

½ cup          soft shortening

½ cup          liquid honey

¼ cup          packed brown sugar

1              egg

½ cup          smooth peanut butter

1 tsp.         vanilla extract

2¼ cups        whole wheat flour

½ tsp.         baking soda

¼ tsp.         salt

Heat oven to 350°F. Have ready ungreased cookie sheets.

Beat shortening, honey, sugar, and egg together until light and fluffy. Beat in peanut butter and vanilla. Stir flour, soda, and salt together with a fork and add to peanut butter mixture, blending well.

Shape dough into small balls, about 1 inch in diameter, and put on cookie sheets. Flatten with the tines of a fork.

Bake 10 to 12 minutes or until set.

Makes about 4 dozen.

# RAISIN-LEMON DROPS 🐝🐝

| | |
|---|---|
| 1 cup | golden raisins |
| ½ cup | soft shortening |
| ½ cup | liquid honey |
| 2 | eggs |
| 2 tsp. | grated lemon rind |
| 3 tbsp. | lemon juice |
| 2 cups | whole wheat flour |
| ¼ tsp. | salt |
| 1 tsp. | baking powder |
| ½ tsp. | baking soda |

Cover raisins with boiling water and let stand 5 minutes. Drain. Heat oven to 375°F. Grease cookie sheets.

Beat shortening, honey, and eggs together until fluffy. Blend in lemon rind and juice. Stir flour, salt, baking powder, and soda together with a fork. Blend into creamed mixture and stir in raisins.

Drop by rounded teaspoonfuls onto prepared cookie sheets. Bake until lightly browned and set, about 15 minutes.

Makes about 3½ dozen.

**Note:** When baking cookies, have oven rack at or just above the middle of the oven for best browning.

## SPONGE CUPCAKES 🍎

| | |
|---|---|
| 1 | large egg |
| ½ cup | sugar |
| 3 tbsp. | orange juice |
| ½ cup | sifted all-purpose flour |
| ½ tsp. | baking powder |
| Pinch | salt |
| 1½ tsp. | grated orange rind |

Heat oven to 375°F. Grease 8 large muffin cups or line them with paper baking cups.

Beat egg in small mixer bowl at high speed on mixer 3 minutes. Beat in sugar gradually, then blend in orange juice. Sift flour, baking powder, and salt together and blend into egg mixture. Fold in orange rind.

Spoon batter into muffin cups or paper cups filling about two-thirds full. Bake about 18 minutes or until tops spring back when touched in the middle. Loosen from pan while hot and cool on rack. Store in a tight tin.

Makes 8.

# LAZY-DAISY CAKE 🍎🍎

| | |
|---|---|
| 2 | eggs |
| 1 cup | sugar |
| 1 tsp. | vanilla extract |
| 1 cup | sifted all-purpose flour |
| 1 tsp. | baking powder |
| Pinch | salt |
| ½ cup | milk |
| 1 tbsp. | butter |
| 3 tbsp. | butter |
| ⅓ cup | packed brown sugar |
| 2 tbsp. | light cream |
| ½ cup | flaked coconut |

Heat oven to 350°F. Grease an 8-inch square cake pan.

Beat eggs well in small mixer bowl. Add sugar gradually and beat well after each addition. Beat in vanilla. Sift flour, baking powder, and salt together and stir into egg mixture. Heat milk to scalding, add 1 tbsp. butter, and stir until butter melts. Add to cake batter, beating until blended. Pour batter into prepared pan.

Bake about 35 minutes or until top springs back when touched lightly in the center. Remove cake from oven and turn on broiler.

Melt 3 tbsp. butter in small saucepan. Stir in brown sugar, cream, and coconut. Drop mixture by small spoonfuls on top of cake and spread carefully. Broil until bubbling and lightly browned. Cool in pan.

# QUICK COTTAGE RICE PUDDING 🐦

| | |
|---|---|
| 3 tbsp. | milk |
| 1 | egg yolk |
| 1 cup | water |
| 1 tbsp. | brown sugar |
| Dash | ground nutmeg |
| 2 tbsp. | seeded raisins |
| 1 cup | precooked long-grain rice (directly from the package) |
| ¼ cup | cottage cheese |
| 2 tbsp. | orange marmalade |
| ¼ tsp. | vanilla extract |

Beat milk and egg yolk together to blend well in a medium saucepan. Add water, sugar, nutmeg, and raisins. Bring to a boil, stirring constantly. Add rice and stir with a fork. Remove from heat, cover pan, and let stand 5 minutes. Stir in cheese, marmalade, and vanilla. Cover again and let stand 5 minutes. Serve warm or cold with cream if desired.

Serves 2 or 3.

## MY FAVORITE APPLE CRISP 🍎

| | |
|---|---|
| 3 | medium cooking apples (e.g., McIntosh, Spy, Spartan) |
| 2 tbsp. | water |
| ½ tsp. | ground cinnamon |
| 2 tbsp. | butter or margarine |
| ⅓ cup | packed brown sugar |
| 3 tbsp. | all-purpose flour |
| 3 tbsp. | quick-cooking rolled oats |
| | Light cream or plain yogurt |

Heat oven to 350°F. Butter a 1-qt. casserole.

Peel, core, and slice apples into prepared casserole. Drizzle with water and sprinkle with cinnamon.

Combine butter or margarine, sugar, flour, and rolled oats, first with a fork, then with fingers, to make a crumbly mixture. Sprinkle over apples and pat down lightly.

Bake about 35 minutes or until apples are tender. (Time depends on the kind of apples you use.) Serve warm or cold with cream or yogurt.

Serves 2.

**To Microwave:** Prepare as above, then microwave at high, uncovered, 10 minutes, turning dish ½ turn after 5 minutes. Let stand 5 minutes and serve. Or cool, chill, and serve cold.

# CHEESE-APPLE CRISP ❦

| 1¼ cups | chopped, peeled apple (1 large) |
| ½ cup | chopped prunes, seeded raisins, or dates |
| 1 tbsp. | water |
| 1 tsp. | lemon juice |
| ¼ cup | sugar |
| ¼ cup | all-purpose flour |
| ½ tsp. | ground cinnamon |
| 2 tbsp. | butter or margarine |
| ¼ cup | grated old cheddar cheese |
| | Cream, ice cream, or yogurt (optional) |

Heat oven to 375 °F. Butter a small casserole (20-oz. size is about right).

Combine apples and your choice of the dried fruit in the casserole and sprinkle with the water and lemon juice.

Mix sugar, flour, and cinnamon, then add butter or margarine and cut in finely. Add cheese and mix lightly with fingers to make a crumbly mixture. Sprinkle over apples and pat down lightly. Bake until apples are tender, about 30 minutes. Serve warm with cream, ice cream, or yogurt if desired.

Serves 2.

# PEAR CRUMBLE 🐛

| | |
|---|---|
| 2 | large fresh pears, peeled and cored |
| 1 tbsp. | lemon juice |
| ½ tsp. | grated lemon rind |
| ¼ cup | coarsely broken walnuts |
| | Nutmeg (optional) |
| ¼ cup | quick-cooking rolled oats |
| ¼ cup | packed brown sugar |
| 2 tbsp. | melted butter or margarine |
| | Plain yogurt (optional) |

Heat oven to 350°F. Butter a small casserole (about 20-oz. size).

Slice pears into casserole, add lemon juice, lemon rind, and walnuts. Toss lightly with a fork and sprinkle with nutmeg.

Combine rolled oats, sugar, and butter or margarine, blending with a fork. Sprinkle over pears. Bake about 30 minutes or until pears are tender and topping is browned. Serve warm, topped with yogurt.

Serves 2.

## OLD-FASHIONED BREAD PUDDING ❦❦

| | |
|---|---|
| 2 cups | bread cubes (bread should be fairly dry) |
| 2 | eggs |
| 1 cup | milk |
| ¼ cup | sugar |
| 1 tsp. | grated lemon rind |
| ¼ cup | seeded raisins (the big, plump ones) |
| | Clear Liquid Sauce (recipe follows) |

Heat oven to 350°F. Butter a small casserole (about 20-oz. size).

Put bread cubes in prepared casserole. Beat eggs, then stir in milk, sugar, lemon rind, and raisins. Pour over bread and let stand until milk is absorbed.

Bake 30 minutes or until set. Serve hot with **Clear Liquid Sauce** poured over top.

Serves 2.

**Note:** Use homemade-type bread if possible.

**Clear Liquid Sauce**

| ¼ cup | sugar |
|-------|-------|
| 1 tsp. | cornstarch |
| ½ cup | boiling water |
| 2 tsp. | butter |
| 1 tbsp. | lemon juice |
| 1 tsp. | vanilla extract |
| | Pinch ground nutmeg |

Mix sugar and cornstarch in a small heavy saucepan. Stir in water gradually, then set over high heat and stir constantly until boiling, slightly thickened and clear. Turn heat to low and cook gently 5 minutes, stirring constantly. Remove from heat and stir in remaining ingredients. Serve hot over pudding.

Makes about ½ cup.

# RHUBARB BROWN BETTY 🍂

| 1 tbsp. | butter or margarine |
| 1½ cups | bread cubes (bread should be fairly dry) |
| ½ cup | sugar |
| 1 tbsp. | grated orange rind |
| ¼ tsp. | ground cinnamon |
| 1½ cups | cut-up rhubarb |
| 2 tbsp. | water |
| 2 tbsp. | orange juice |
| | Light cream |

Heat oven to 375 °F. Butter a 1-qt. casserole.

Melt butter or margarine in a small saucepan. Add bread cubes and toss together until cubes are coated with butter. Mix sugar, orange rind, and cinnamon.

Put a third of the bread cubes in the bottom of the casserole. Add half the rhubarb and half the sugar mixture. Repeat these layers and end with a final layer of bread cubes. Sprinkle in the water and orange juice. Cover.

Bake 35 minutes, then uncover and continue baking about 10 minutes or until rhubarb is tender and top is lightly browned. Serve with cream.

Serves 2.

## BAKED PRUNE WHIP 🦌🦌

| ½ cup | finely cut-up cooked prunes |
| 2 | egg whites |
| 3 tbsp. | sugar |
| Pinch | salt |
| 2 tsp. | lemon juice |
| ¼ tsp. | vanilla extract |
| 2 tbsp. | chopped pecans (optional) |
| | Soft Custard (page 228) |

Heat oven to 350 °F. Have ready two 6-oz. custard cups. Put a pan of hot water large enough to hold the custard cups in the oven (have water 1-inch deep).

Beat prunes, egg whites, sugar, and salt until stiff enough to hold shape. Fold in lemon juice, vanilla, and pecans. Spoon into custard cups (they will be very full) and set in the pan of hot water.

Bake until puffed and lightly browned, about 20 minutes. Serve hot or cold with **Soft Custard**.

Serves 2.

**Note:** To cook prunes, cover with cold water in saucepan, bring to a boil, and simmer until very tender, about 20 minutes. Cool, drain, and cut up with kitchen scissors.

# CHEESE LAYERS ❦

| | |
|---|---|
| 1 cup | 2% cottage cheese |
| 2 tbsp. | sugar |
| 1 tsp. | vanilla extract |
| ½ cup | graham wafer crumbs |
| 2 tbsp. | melted butter or margarine |
| ⅛ tsp. | ground cinnamon |
| | Fresh fruit |

Press cottage cheese through a sieve or process in food processor until smooth. Stir in sugar and vanilla. Combine graham wafer crumbs, butter or margarine, and cinnamon.

Layer cottage cheese mixture and graham wafer crumbs in parfait glasses or goblets, making as many layers as possible. Chill until serving time. Top with fruit.

Serves 2.

# BANANA CUSTARD 🍎

| | |
|---|---|
| ¼ cup | skim milk |
| 1⅓ cups | plain skim milk yogurt or 2 cartons (175 g each) regular plain yogurt |
| 1 | medium, very ripe banana |
| 3¼-oz. (92 g) pkg. | instant vanilla pudding mix |
| ½ tsp. | almond extract |
| 2 tbsp. | toasted wheat germ |

Put milk, yogurt, banana, pudding mix, and almond extract in the blender and blend until smooth. Spoon half into 4 sherbet glasses or custard cups. Sprinkle with half the wheat germ, add remaining pudding, cover, and chill. At serving time sprinkle with remaining wheat germ.

Makes 4 small servings.

## EGG WHITE CUSTARD 🐞🐞

| | |
|---|---|
| 1 | egg white |
| ¼ tsp. | vanilla extract |
| 1½ tbsp. | sugar |
| ⅔ cup | whole milk |
| | Rum-Raspberry Sauce (recipe follows) |

Heat oven to 325°F. Have ready two 6-oz. custard cups. Put a pan of hot water large enough to hold the custard cups in the oven (have water 1-inch deep).

Beat egg white and vanilla with an electric mixer or rotary beater until foamy. Add sugar a little at a time, beating well after each addition. Beat until stiff.

Scald milk and add it slowly to the beaten egg white, beating at low speed until blended. Pour into custard cups (they will be very full) and set them in the pan of hot water in the oven. Bake until a knife inserted near the center comes out clean, about 40 minutes. Cool, cover with transparent wrap and chill well.

Unmold at serving time (custard will be quite soft) and spoon **Rum-Raspberry Sauce** over each.

Serves 2.

## Rum-Raspberry Sauce

| ¼ cup | seedless raspberry jam |
| 2 tbsp. | water |
| ¾ tsp. | cornstarch |
| 2 tsp. | golden rum |

Heat jam and 1 tbsp. water to boiling. Combine remaining water and cornstarch, stirring until smooth. Stir into boiling mixture gradually. Cook stirring, until boiling and thickened. Remove from heat and stir in rum. Cool then chill.

Makes ⅓ cup.

**Note:** If you have your own frozen raspberries, make the sauce with 1 cup of them. Heat raspberries and 1 tbsp. water to boiling, then press through a sieve to remove the seeds and thicken as directed. If you can't find seedless jam, press the boiling jam through a sieve to remove seeds before thickening.

# INDIVIDUAL DATE PUDDINGS (STEAMED) ❧❧❧

| | |
|---|---|
| 3 tbsp. | butter or margarine |
| ½ cup | packed brown sugar |
| 1 | egg |
| 1¼ cups | sifted all-purpose flour |
| 1 tsp. | baking powder |
| ½ tsp. | baking soda |
| ¼ tsp. | salt |
| ½ tsp. | ground cinnamon |
| ½ cup | milk |
| ½ tsp. | vanilla extract |
| ¾ cup | chopped dates |
| ½ cup | chopped walnuts |
| 1 tsp. | grated lemon rind |

Cream butter or margarine and sugar. Add egg, beating well. Sift flour, baking powder, soda, salt, and cinnamon together. Add to creamed mixture alternately with milk and vanilla. Fold in dates, walnuts, and lemon rind. Spoon into 6 well-greased 6-oz. custard cups. Cover each cup tightly with foil. Set on a rack in a large kettle, add 1 inch boiling water, cover kettle tightly and steam 1 hour.

Cool puddings, wrap each in foil, and store in a cool place or freeze. Steam again 30 minutes at serving time. **Lemon Sauce** (page 227) is good with this pudding.

Makes 6 small puddings.

# BUTTERSCOTCH-APPLE PARFAITS 🍎🍎

| | |
|---|---|
| 4-oz. pkg. | butterscotch pudding mix (the kind you cook) |
| 2 | egg whites |
| ¼ cup | sugar |
| ¼ tsp. | vanilla extract |
| 1 | medium unpeeled apple, finely grated (¾ to 1 cup) |
| ½ cup | crushed peanut brittle |

Prepare pudding mix as directed on package. Chill quickly by setting in ice water and stirring constantly.

Beat egg whites until foamy, add sugar gradually, beating well after each addition and continuing beating until stiff peaks form. Beat in vanilla, then fold in apple.

Layer butterscotch pudding and the apple-egg white mixture in 4 large sherbet glasses or goblets, sprinkling each layer of egg white mixture with a little of the peanut brittle. Serve immediately or chill no longer than 1 hour.

Makes 4 servings.

# EASY INDIVIDUAL TRIFLES 🦌🦌

| | |
|---|---|
| 1⅓ cups | plain yogurt |
| 2 tbsp. | liquid honey |
| ½ tsp. | vanilla extract |
| 4 | Sponge Cupcakes (page 198) |
| 1 tbsp. | sherry |
| 2 tbsp. | raspberry jam |
| 2 tbsp. | chopped, toasted almonds |
| | Whipped cream (optional) |

Put yogurt in a small bowl and stir in honey and vanilla.

Line bottom and sides of 2 large sherbet glasses or goblets (about 10-oz. size) with pieces of cake cut ¼-inch thick. (Depending on the shape of the glass, this will take 1½ to 2 cupcakes for each trifle.) Drizzle cake with sherry and spread with jam. Pour in the yogurt and sprinkle with almonds.

Chill about 1 hour or until serving time. Top with whipped cream if desired.

Serves 2.

# BAKED APPLE SLICES ❦

| | |
|---|---|
| 3 | medium cooking apple |
| 1 tbsp. | soft butter or margarine |
| ¼ cup | sugar |
| ⅛ tsp. | ground cinnamon |
| Pinch | ground nutmeg |
| 3 tbsp. | light cream |

Heat oven to 350 °F. Butter a 1-qt. casserole.

Peel, core, and slice apples into prepared casserole. Dot with butter or margarine and sprinkle with a mixture of the sugar and spices. Pour cream over all. Cover and bake until apples are tender, about 30 minutes, stirring once with a fork. Serve warm or cold.

Serves 2.

**To Microwave:** Combine ingredients in casserole and cover with waxed paper. Microwave at high 6 minutes or until apples are tender, stirring after 4 minutes.

## ...ED APPLES 🐛

| | |
|---|---|
| 2 | baking apples |
| ¼ cup | brown sugar |
| 2 tbsp. | raisins |
| ¼ tsp. | ground cinnamon |
| ½ tsp. | grated lemon rind |
| 1 tsp. | butter |
| ¼ cup | water |
| | Light cream (optional) |

Heat oven to 350°F. Have ready a small baking dish large enough to hold the apples.

Core the apples and peel them a third of the way down from the top. Set in the baking dish and fill centers with a mixture of sugar, raisins, cinnamon, and lemon rind. Dot with butter. Pour water around the apples and bake 30 to 40 minutes until just tender. Serve warm with cream if desired.

Serves 2.

**To Microwave:** Put apples in custard cups, cover with waxed paper and microwave at high 4 to 5½ minutes or until tender. (Cooking time depends on the kind of apples.) Let stand 10 minutes.

# APPLESAUCE 🍎🍎

| 4 | medium red cooking apples |
|---|---|
| 3 tbsp. | water |
| 2 tbsp. | maple syrup |

Wash, quarter, and core apples. Put in a saucepan with the water. Bring to a boil over high heat, reduce heat to medium, cover and simmer until apples are breaking up, 12 to 15 minutes. Stir in maple syrup.

Remove from heat and press apple pulp through a sieve, discarding skins. Makes about 1½ cups.

**Note:** You may use 3 tbsp. granulated sugar or 2 tbsp. brown sugar or honey for the sweetener if you prefer. Add ¼ tsp. cinnamon, ⅛ tsp. nutmeg, and a pinch of cloves if you like a spicy applesauce.

**To Microwave:** Put apples and water in 1-qt. casserole, cover, and microwave at high 6 minutes or until very tender. Stir in sweetener and press through a sieve as directed in recipe.

## APPLE FLOWERS 🍎

| | |
|---|---|
| 2 | baking apples |
| 4 tsp. | red currant jelly |
| 2 cubes (½-inch) | cream cheese |
| 1 tsp. | butter or margarine |

Heat oven to 350°F. Have ready a baking dish just large enough to hold the apples.

Core apples from stem end, leaving the blossom end intact to hold the filling. Do not peel apples. Cut each apple into 6 wedges from the top to about half way down toward the bottom. Put 2 tsp. jelly in each apple and add a cube of cheese, pushing it well down into the cavity. Add ½ tsp. butter or margarine to each apple.

Set apples in the baking dish and add about 2 tbsp. water to the bottom of the dish. Bake about 30 minutes or until apples are just tender but not breaking up. Serve warm.

Serves 2.

# GINGER FRUIT 🦫🦫

| ¾ cup | canned pineapple chunks, drained |
| 2 tbsp. | pineapple juice |
| 1 | orange |
| ½ | grapefruit |
| 1 | tangerine (or ⅓ cup canned mandarin orange sections, drained) |
| 1 tbsp. | liquid honey |
| 1 tbsp. | finely chopped preserved ginger (sometimes called ginger in syrup) |

Put pineapple and juice in a bowl. Peel orange, cutting away all white under the skin, then section (hold fruit over bowl to catch the juice), cutting the pulp away from the dividing membranes and letting the sections drop into the bowl. Scoop the sections out of the half grapefruit into the bowl with a spoon, squeezing all juice into the bowl. Peel and separate sections of tangerine, stripping off connective membranes and removing seeds. (You can eliminate this step if you use canned orange sections.) Add to bowl along with honey and stir well. Let stand 30 minutes at room temperature, stirring often.

Drain all juice from fruit into a saucepan. Add ginger, bring to a boil, and boil hard until there is only about ⅓ cup juice left. Cool (the juice will now be quite syrupy). Pour over fruit, stir, cover, and chill. Serve in chilled sherbet glasses.

Serves 2.

**Note:** Use pineapple that is canned in its own juice — no sugar added.

# KIWI AND BANANA ❦

| ⅓ cup | low-fat plain yogurt |
| 1 tbsp. | brown sugar |
| ¼ tsp. | grated lime rind |
| 1 tsp. | coffee liqueur (optional) |
| 1 | kiwi fruit |
| 1 | ripe banana |
| 1 tbsp. | toasted coconut |

Combine yogurt, sugar, lime rind, and liqueur. Chill well. At serving time, peel fruit and slice half the kiwi fruit and half the banana into each of 2 serving dishes. Top each with a large spoonful of yogurt mixture and sprinkle with coconut. Serve immediately.

Serves 2.

**Note:** To toast coconut, put on foil in a 350°F oven for about 2 minutes, stirring once or twice. Watch carefully; coconut should be golden not dark brown. The toaster oven is useful for little jobs like this.

## MANDARIN YOGURT ❧

| ½ cup | canned mandarin oranges, drained |
| 1⅓ cups | peach or apricot yogurt (or 2 cartons—175 g each) |
| ½ tsp. | almond extract |
| 1 tbsp. | toasted slivered almonds |

Dry orange sections well on paper towelling. Set 4 sections aside to use as garnish and fold the remaining sections, yogurt, and almond extract together. Spoon the mixture into sherbet glasses and garnish each with a few almond slivers and 2 orange sections. Chill until serving time.

Serves 2.

## ORANGE SLICES WITH CINNAMON ❧

| 2 | oranges |
| 2 tsp. | sugar |
| ½ tsp. | ground cinnamon |

Peel oranges and cut in thick slices. Spread the slices in 2 serving dishes. Mix the sugar and cinnamon and sprinkle a little of the mixture over each serving.

Serves 2.

# HOT PEACHES 🦌🦌

| | |
|---|---|
| 2 tbsp. | butter or margarine |
| ½ cup | ½-inch cubes day-old white bread |
| 2 tbsp. | brown sugar |
| ¼ tsp. | ground nutmeg |
| 2 | medium peaches, peeled and cubed |
| | Ice cream |

Melt butter or margarine in a small skillet. Add bread cubes and cook gently, stirring, until golden. Add sugar and nutmeg and stir over medium heat until bread cubes are sugary-crisp. Add peaches and cook gently, stirring, 2 minutes. Put a scoop of ice cream in 2 serving dishes and spoon the hot mixture over. Serve immediately.

Serves 2.

**Note:** Prepare peaches at serving time. If they are nice and ripe, the skin should peel off easily. Then make a cut right around the peach and cut in thick slices the other direction so large pieces fall off the pit.

# SPICED PEARS 🍃🍃

| | |
|---|---|
| 19-oz. can | pear halves |
| ⅓ cup | fresh orange juice |
| 1 tbsp. | lemon juice |
| ⅛ tsp. | ground ginger |
| ½ | cinnamon stick |
| 2 | whole cloves |
| ½ cup | red currant jelly |
| | Red food coloring (optional) |
| ⅔ cup | plain yogurt |
| 2 tsp. | sugar |
| ½ tsp. | vanilla extract |

Drain pears, saving juice. Combine pear juice, orange juice, lemon juice, ginger, cinnamon, and cloves in a small saucepan. Bring to a boil, reduce heat, and simmer, uncovered, 10 minutes. Put pears in a small deep bowl and pour the hot juice over. Let stand 1 hour at room temperature, then chill.

Beat jelly with a rotary beater until smooth at serving time. Add 1 tbsp. of the spiced pear juice and a few drops of red food coloring to brighten the red color and beat to blend. Combine yogurt, sugar, and vanilla.

Lift pear halves out of juice and put them in sherbet glasses. Top each serving with a spoonful of the jelly, then a spoonful of yogurt. Serve immediately.

Makes 4 servings.

**Note:** The juice left from the pears makes a good liquid to use with a jelly powder for dessert another day.

# SPICED PINEAPPLE AND BLUEBERRIES ❦

| | |
|---|---|
| 14-oz. can | pineapple chunks (in own juice) |
| 1 tbsp. | lemon juice |
| 1 | small stick cinnamon |
| 2 | whole cloves |
| 1 tsp. | vanilla extract |
| 1 cup | fresh or frozen blueberries |

Drain pineapple and heat ⅔ cup of the juice to boiling along with lemon juice, cinnamon, and cloves. Simmer 5 minutes. Remove from heat and add vanilla and pineapple chunks. Cool, stirring often. Cover and chill well. Thaw frozen blueberries and drain well.

Remove and discard cinnamon stick and cloves at serving time. Spoon pineapple and some of the syrup into large sherbet glasses and sprinkle generously with blueberries.

Makes 4 servings.

# PRUNE COMPOTE ❧

| 12-oz. pkg. | pitted prunes |
| 3 slices | unpeeled lemon, cut into quarters |
| 3 slices | unpeeled orange, cut into quarters |
| ¼ cup | seedless raisins |
| 1 stick | cinnamon, broken |
| ¼ tsp. | ground nutmeg |
| | Cold water |

Combine prunes, lemon and orange pieces, raisins, cinnamon, and nutmeg in a 1-qt. jar. Cover with cold water, then cover jar and store in the refrigerator 5 days before serving.

Makes 6 servings.

# STRAWBERRIES WITH YOGURT TOPPING ❧

| ½ cup | plain yogurt |
| 1 tbsp. | liquid honey |
| Pinch | ground cardamom |
| 1 pint | strawberries |

Stir yogurt, honey, and cardamom to blend and chill until serving time. Divide berries into 2 serving dishes and spoon the yogurt over top.

Serves 2.

## DRIED FRUIT COMPOTE 🍎

| 8 oz. pkg. | mixed dried fruit |
| 1 cup | dry white wine |
| ⅔ cup | orange juice |
| ¼ tsp. | ground cinnamon |
| 1 | whole clove |

Bring all ingredients to a boil in a medium saucepan over medium heat. Cover, reduce heat, and simmer until fruit is tender, about 35 minutes. Cool and chill.

Makes 4 servings.

**Note:** Packages of mixed fruit contain dried apples, pears, peaches, apricots, and prunes.

# LEMON SAUCE ❦

| ½ cup  | sugar              |
|--------|--------------------|
| 1 tbsp. | cornstarch        |
| 2 tbsp. | lemon juice       |
| ⅔ cup  | boiling water      |
| 1 tsp. | grated lemon rind  |
| ½ tsp. | grated orange rind |
| 1 tsp. | butter             |

Combine sugar and cornstarch thoroughly in a small saucepan. Stir in lemon juice and boiling water gradually. Set over high heat and bring to a boil, stirring constantly. Reduce heat and boil gently 1 minute. Remove from heat and stir in lemon and orange rind and butter. Serve warm. (Good over steamed puddings, baked apples, etc.)

Makes about ⅔ cup.

## ORANGE-BANANA SAUCE ❦

| | |
|---|---|
| 1 | medium orange, peeled and diced |
| 1 | small ripe banana, peeled and diced |
| 1 tbsp. | water |
| 1½ tsp. | liquid honey |
| 1½ tsp. | cornstarch |
| 2 tbsp. | water |

Combine orange and banana pieces, 1 tbsp. water, and honey in a small saucepan and bring to a boil. Combine cornstarch and 2 tbsp. water, stirring until smooth, then stir into boiling fruit mixture and cook over medium heat until slightly thickened and clear. Cool. Serve over ice cream, custard, etc.

Makes about ⅔ cup.

## SOFT CUSTARD ❦

| | |
|---|---|
| ¾ cup | milk |
| 2 | egg yolks |
| 2 tbsp. | sugar |
| 1 tsp. | vanilla extract |

Scald milk in top of double boiler over direct heat. Beat egg yolks in a small bowl, blend in the sugar, and gradually stir in the hot milk. Put mixture in the top of the double boiler and set over simmering water. Stir constantly until mixture coats a metal spoon, about 10 minutes. Cool quickly by setting in ice water. Stir in vanilla and chill. Serve over fruit.

Makes ¾ cup.

# PASTRY FOR 2-CRUST 9-INCH PIE

| 2 cups | sifted all-purpose flour |
| 1 tsp. | salt |
| ⅔ cup | pure lard (or ¾ cup vegetable shortening) |
| ¼ cup | ice water |

Put flour in a bowl. Add salt and stir lightly with a fork. Add shortening and cut in coarsely with a pastry blender (pieces should be about the size of peas). Sprinkle in water 1 tbsp. at a time, tossing with a fork just until flour is dampened. Don't stir. Try not to add more water even though dough looks a little dry. Gather dough into a ball and press together firmly, handling as little as possible. Divide into 2 pieces and shape each into a flattened round.

Roll 1 round on floured pastry cloth, rolling lightly from the center out rather than back and forth. Roll to ⅛-inch thickness, stopping and rounding up dough occasionally. If dough tears or cracks, trim off a little from the edge and use it to mend the tear or crack by rolling it on. Roll pastry around rolling pin and lift it into the pie pan. Fit it in loosely and press it into place so no air is trapped underneath. Add filling and trim off overhang.

Roll other piece of pastry in the same way, moisten edge of lower pastry, and lift top pastry into place. Seal to bottom pastry and trim to ½ inch from edge of pie pan. Roll edge of top pastry under edge of bottom pastry on rim of pan, sealing well. Flute edge by putting your index finger on the inside of the pastry edge and pressing it between the other index finger and thumb on the outside, pinching each flute.

Cover the edge with a narrow strip of foil to keep it from browning too much and cut a large slit in the top to let the steam escape. Bake according to recipe.

For 1-crust 9-inch pie: make half the recipe, line pan as directed, and roll edge under and flute. Hook points of flutes under rim of pie pan to keep pastry from shrinking. Fill and bake according to recipe. Or, if you wish to fill after baking, prick all over with the tines of a fork and bake at 475°F 8 to 10 minutes or until brown.

# CRUMB PIE SHELLS

For really easy crusts for pies, nothing can beat crumb crusts. Here are directions for several of them. You can of course, make half the mixture and press it into foil tart pans for small pies. These crusts are quite good simply filled with packaged pie fillings.

### Bread Crumb Pie Shell

| | |
|---|---|
| ¾ cup | fine dry bread crumbs |
| ⅓ cup | packed brown sugar |
| ¼ cup | butter or margarine, melted |
| ½ tsp. | ground cinnamon |

### Vanilla, Chocolate, or Ginger Crumb Pie Shell

| | |
|---|---|
| 1½ cups | finely crushed vanilla, chocolate or ginger wafers |
| ⅓ cup | butter or margarine, melted |

### Corn Flake Pie Shell

| | |
|---|---|
| 1½ cups | fine corn flake crumbs |
| ¼ cup | butter or margarine, melted |
| 2 tbsp. | sugar |

Heat oven to 350 °F. Have ready a 9-inch pie pan.

For each of these variations, blend ingredients well and press firmly on bottom and sides of pie pan, building up as high an edge as possible. Bake 10 minutes, then cool.

## LEMON-CHEESE PIE 🐞🐞

| | |
|---|---|
| 1 cup | vanilla wafer crumbs (about 28 wafers) |
| 3 tbsp. | butter or margarine, melted |
| 2 tsp. | sugar |
| 2 tsp. | lemon juice |
| 125 g pkg. | cream cheese at room temperature |
| 2 tbsp. | lemon juice |
| 1 | egg |
| ⅓ cup | sugar |
| ¼ cup | commercial sour cream |
| 1 tsp. | sugar |
| 1 tsp. | grated lemon rind |

Heat oven to 350°F. Lightly grease 2 small (4½ x 1¼-inch) foil tart pans. Combine vanilla wafer crumbs, butter or margarine, 2 tsp. sugar and 2 tsp. lemon juice, mixing well with a fork. Press evenly and firmly over bottom and sides of pans.

Beat cream cheese with rotary beater until fluffy. Blend in 2 tbsp. lemon juice. Add egg and beat well. Gradually beat in ⅓ cup sugar. Pour into crumb crusts and bake 20 minutes. Remove from oven and cool 5 minutes.

Combine sour cream, 1 tsp. sugar, and lemon rind and spread over cheese mixture. Bake 10 minutes. Cool, then chill several hours. Cut in small pieces to serve.

Each pie serves 2 or 4.

# MENUS

I often hear people say they don't mind cooking but they wish someone else would plan the meals. So I thought some menu suggestions might be useful. Even if you don't use the menus just as they appear here, I hope you'll find they make a good guide as to what to serve with what. I've planned them so, where possible, they include something from each of the food groups recommended by Canada's Food Guide, so they should be healthful as well as good to eat.

Most of the recipes serve two, but some make four servings, so you may find you have to adjust the amounts to fit the menu in a few cases.

There are recipes in this book for most of the dishes that appear in the menus. You'll find them easily by looking in the Index.

## BREAKFAST

Fresh Orange Juice
Whole Wheat Pancakes with Hot Applesauce
Small Breakfast Sausages (two per person)
Coffee with Hot Milk


Orange Eggnog
Corn Flakes
Cinnamon Toast


Tomato Juice
Poached Eggs On Whole Wheat Toast
Bran Muffins
Coffee or Tea


Apple Flowers
Whole Wheat Toast with Sharp Cheese Spread
Cocoa


Mixed Grapefruit and Orange Sections
Apple-flavored Hot Cereal
Blueberry Muffins
Coffee or Tea


Orange Slices with Cinnamon
French Toast with Maple Syrup
Crisp Bacon
Coffee

Strawberries with Yogurt Topping
Ham Omelet
Toasted English Muffins
Tea


Prune Compote
Finnan Haddie with Egg Sauce
Whole wheat toast
Marmalade
Coffee

## LUNCH OR SUPPER

Corned Beef Patties
Lettuce Wedge with Sesame Dressing
Dried Fruit Compote


Chicken and Melon Salad
Whole Wheat Ribbons
Sherbet and Cookies
Minted Iced Tea


Puffy Tuna Sandwiches
Easy Summer Salad
Kiwi and Banana
Raisin Lemon Drops


Clear Celery Soup
Creamed Salmon on Toast
Sliced Tomatoes
Quick Cottage Rice Pudding

Plain Macaroni and Cheese
Lettuce-pickle Slaw
Rye Bread
Ginger Fruit
Honey Peanut Butter Cookies


Mulligatawny
Grilled Cheese Sandwiches
Sweet Pickles
Apples and Cookies


Steak Soup
No-knead Oatmeal Bread
Fresh Fruit


Quick Vegetable Chowder
Country Cottage Sandwiches
Rhubarb Brown Betty


Corn Chowder
Ham and Slaw Pita Pockets
Baked Apples


**DINNER**

Yankee Pot Roast
Noodles
Savory Carrots
Lettuce Wedge with Citrus Peanut Dressing
My Favorite Apple Crisp

Golden Sole
Parsley Boiled Potatoes
Broiled Tomatoes
Carrot Sprout Salad
Ice Cream or Lemon Sherbet with Orange Banana
Sauce


Lamb Chops with Potatoes
Peas in Cream
Zucchini and Tomato Salad
Egg White Custard
Rum Raspberry Sauce


Mushroom Consommé
Creamy Macaroni and Cheese
Tossed Green Salad
Corn Bread
Fruit


Quick Corn Soup
Ground Beef and Noodles
Coleslaw
Banana Custard


Salmon and Rice Casserole
Avocado-Orange Salad
Hot Biscuits
Cheese Layers

Chicken in Spicy Orange Sauce
Baked Brown Rice
Butter-Steamed Broccoli
Mushroom Salad
Fruit
Lazy-Daisy Cake


Stuffed Chicken Breast
Fruited Rice
Butter-Steamed Zucchini
Easy Individual Trifles


Italian Stew, Hunter's Style
Orange and Onion Salad
Hot French Bread
Bananas with Soft Custard


Gazpacho
Veal Cutlets Tarragon
Baked Barley and Mushrooms
Fresh Asparagus
Mandarin Yogurt


Spicy Tomato Bouillon
Steak Roast
Baked Potatoes
Plain Fried Vegetables
Green and Red Cabbage Slaw
Lemon-Cheese Pie

Oven Fried Fish
Brown Rice
Caesar Salad
Strawberries
Butterscotch-Oat Squares


Blender Cucumber-Beet Soup
Fish Rolls
Rice
Glazed Baby Carrots
Tossed Green Salad
Sherbet


Lamb Loaf
Scalloped Potatoes
Scalloped Tomatoes
Lettuce Wedges with French Dressing
Pear Crumble


Baked Pork Chops and Apples
Noodles
Tossed Green Salad
Quick Mustard-Bean Pickles
Old-Fashioned Bread Pudding
Clear Liquid Sauce


Steak Pie
Herbed Lima Beans
Baked Prune Whip
Soft Custard

# INDEX

245

253

256

258

# OTHER TITLES IN THE
# SELF-COUNSEL
# RETIREMENT SERIES

## MOBILE RETIREMENT HANDBOOK
*A complete guide to living and traveling in an RV*
The author provides many helpful tips on choosing
the right RV, drawing up a budget for both money
and time, preparing to leave your home, and organiz-
ing a network of friends while you're on the road.

*"This handbook will answer your questions on whether
retirement in an RV is right for you. Anyone contemplat-
ing the pleasures of this lifestyle should have this book."*
John Gedak, President, Get-Away Enterprises Inc.

$9.95, 256 pages

## WISE AND HEALTHY LIVING
*A commonsense approach to aging well*
Retirement years can be full of activity and happy
times if approached with a positive attitude and a
willingness to make minor changes to adapt to
changing physical and psychological needs. This
book presents a holistic approach to aging and health.
It discusses the aging process and the changes to be
expected, how to deal with change, and how it may
affect the way you live.

$8.95, 120 pages

## FIT AFTER FIFTY
*Feel better  Live longer*
This book explains the importance of exercise, the effects of aging on how you exercise, how to exercise, precautions to take, special considerations for those with particular health problems, and perhaps most important, the great variety of enjoyable activities that qualify as exercise.

$8.95, 160 pages


## RETIREMENT GUIDE FOR CANADIANS
*An overall plan for a comfortable future*
The years after 65 can be very rewarding, not full of the problems and disappointments that so many retirees experience.  Retirement is another stage in your life and, by careful planning, you can make this stage full and financially stable.  This manual has been written for you by someone who has experienced many of the problems you may encounter, and its aim is to answer as many questions as possible.

$9.95, 284 pages


## U.S. RETIREMENT GUIDE
Will be available in the Spring of 1990.

## PLANNING FOR FINANCIAL INDEPENDENCE
*Choose your lifestyle  Secure your future*
Achieving financial independence is rarely a matter
of luck or speculation. Most often it is the result of
good planning and a sound program of capital ac-
cumulation. Using the conventional tools of investment and savings, the author has developed an array
of financial management techniques that allow his
clients to make long-term financial plans that reflect
their lifestyles and guarantee them the standard of
living they desire.

$11.95, 128 pages


Yes, please send me:

_____ copies of MOBILE RETIREMENT
HANDBOOK, $9.95

_____ copies of WISE AND HEALTHY LIVING
$8.95

_____ copies of FIT AFTER FIFTY, $8.95

_____ copies of RETIREMENT GUIDE FOR
CANADIANS, $9.95

_____ copies of U.S. RETIREMENT GUIDE, $9.95

_____ copies of PLANNING FOR FINANCIAL
INDEPENDENCE, $11.95


There is a $2.50 charge for postage and handling.

Washington residents please add 7.8% sales tax.

# ORDER FORM

All prices subject to change without notice.  Books are available in book and department stores, or use this order form.

(Please print)

Name _____

Address _____

_____

Charge to:

        ❑Visa        ❑MasterCard

Account Number _____

Validation Date _____Expiry Date _____

Checks and money orders accepted.

❑**Check here for a free catalogue which outlines all of our publications.**

**IN CANADA**
Please send your order to the nearest location:

Self-Counsel Press        Self-Counsel Press
1481 Charlotte Road     2399 Cawthra Road, Unit 25
North Vancouver, B.C.   Mississauga, Ont.
V7J 1H1               L5A 2W9

**IN THE U.S.A.**
Please send your order to:

Self-Counsel Press Inc.
1704 N. State Street
Bellingham, WA  98225